DREXLER / SIBBET

# team
PERFORMANCE™

SYSTEM

# team
# leader
# guide

## strategies and practices for
## achieving high performance

TEAM PERFORMANCE SYSTEM

# Introduction to Team Leadership

The *Team Leader Guide: Strategies and Practices* is a compilation of frameworks, strategies and best practices for leaders of work teams. Whether you are new in the role or have been a team leader for a while, you will find the guide full of practical information and helpful suggestions. It will also be useful to self-managed teams looking for support for their operations.

The guide emerges from a decade of work David Sibbet and Allan Drexler devoted to developing the Drexler/Sibbet Team Performance System in the 1980s, and subsequent application to all kinds of teams—from leadership to manufacturing to sales and technical teams. The best practices have emerged from over 30 years of work by The Grove Consultants International in sup-

porting collaborative work in organizations. Ed Claassen, lead author of this guide, brings his years of experience as a senior human resources professional to the work, most especially 12 years as head of training and development at SRI International in Menlo Park, California, and 10 years as a senior consultant with The Grove. His encouragement led to the articulation of 12 success strategies for combining practices in response to repeating, classic challenges team leaders face.

Although the Team Performance Model and best practices described here are supported by considerable research in group process, the intent of this guide is to provide a practical tool for team leadership. We trust you will find it useful.

Published by
THE GROVE CONSULTANTS
INTERNATIONAL
1000 O'Reilly Avenue
San Francisco, CA 94129–1124
Copyright ©2003 The Grove Consultants International

ISBN: 1–879502–53–6

Printed in the USA
Version 1.0, December 2003

Arrangements for special publication and reduced rates for bulk orders are available from:
The Grove Consultants International
1000 O'Reilly Avenue
San Francisco, CA 94129–1124
You can also order online at **www.grove.com**.

# Table of Contents

# Acknowledgements

This *Team Leader Guide* would not have been possible without the involvement of countless people and teams who have worked with the Drexler/Sibbet Team Performance™ System and The Grove's approaches to graphically facilitating group process. We cannot acknowledge all of them, but we can single out a few for special thanks.

This entire work builds on the system for thinking about team performance that came from the collaboration of Allan Drexler and David Sibbet during the 1980s. Allan's extensive experience with manufacturing teams, National Training Labs, and work with Jack Gibb and Marvin Weisbord in the 1970s provided a background in field experience and group process research. David's in-depth experience with Arthur M. Young's Theory of Process and large and small group facilitation rounded out the collaboration. Since then both Drexler and Sibbet have applied their system extensively in the United States and internationally. It includes the Team Performance Model (TPM), a Team Performance Inventory, several books, an abstract, and various workplace learning aids.

As Thom Sibbet, head of The Grove's product division, worked to support the growing number of TPM users and clients, he became increasingly aware of the need for additional support for using the body of best practices. Ed Claassen, The Grove's director of R&D and long-time senior consultant, saw that providing some guidance in the application of these practices by defining success strategies would be very helpful for new team leaders.

An immediate catalyst to developing a new guide came through The Grove's extensive work in leadership development with Agilent Technologies, the business that spun off from Hewlett-Packard in the 1990s. Christine Landon and Pat Chapman Ross, and then Teresa Roche, as stewards of the programs that supported new team leaders at Agilent, invited the application of the Team Performance Model and The Grove's Best Practice guides to their first line manager training program launched in early 2003. Their input regarding relevant practices and integration of a dispersed team's framework was very helpful.

For the product you are now holding, thanks to Bobby Pardini, director of The Grove's Design Solutions Group, for heading the production team, and to Judy Yu for her work producing the final product.

Ed Claassen and David Sibbet

# Section I:

## Understanding Team Leadership

- Welcome to Team Leadership

- Team Leadership—Burden or Opportunity?

- Tools You'll Find in This Guide

- Team Leadership Framework

- Is Your Group a Team?

- What Type of Team Are You Leading?

- The Drexler/Sibbet Team Performance™ Model

- Why Teams Fail

- When to Go for Full Collaboration

# Welcome to Team Leadership

## *Learning the Strategies and Practices of Effective Team Performance*

The growing complexity of organizations, customers, markets and technology means that much of the critical work of organizations can no longer be performed by individuals working separately. Name just about any important issue that your organization faces, and consider the number and range of people needed to formulate a meaningful response. Forming teams to address these issues has become an essential strategy for bringing all the needed perspectives together. Teams have become the core working elements of today's organization.

### Teams Are No Guarantee of Effective Collaboration

If you have experience with teams, you know that forming a team does not guarantee the team will effectively apply its collective knowledge and skills. Everyone can cite examples of teams that have failed to deliver on their charters or expected business results. Put a difficult challenge together with the complex dynamics of a group of people under stress and the chances are high that things will not go as planned.

### Moving Beyond Individual Contributor

If you are a team leader, you are probably charged with the responsibility of guiding the work of your team and dealing with these challenges. You were probably chosen as one of the more knowledgeable, experienced members of your group or you may be on a self-managed team charged to find ways to improve itself. In either case, it is important to understand that the skills and knowledge that made you a successful individual contributor will not, by themselves, make you a successful team leader.

As ***team leader,*** your success and effectiveness is based more on your ability to guide the work of others than the individual results you contribute. This guide offers the framework and tools to help you succeed in this role.

## How Do You Think About Teamwork?

Read the list of challenges in the box on the right. Ask yourself what strikes you as the biggest challenge for you personally as a team leader. Is it addressing the complexity of the work itself? Or is it molding a group of individuals into a fully aligned and committed team? Clearly both are critical elements of success. The task-related challenges require your best professional knowledge, experience and leadership. The people-related challenges require that you also step into the role of facilitator and team-process guide, a role that is very different from that of experienced individual contributor that you probably know best.

### TEAM LEADER RESPONSIBILITIES

As team leader you are responsible for ensuring that your team accomplishes its goals. Your challenge is to:

#### Set Direction

☐ Ensure that all the members of your team understand and endorse the purpose for which the team has been assembled.

☐ Translate the purpose into clear goals and objectives for your team as a whole.

#### Facilitate Relationships

☐ Establish the working relationships necessary for your team members to actively engage each other in accomplishing the goals of the team.

☐ Help your team establish a pattern of success and overcome unanticipated difficulties.

#### Develop Capabilities

☐ Support all your team members in setting individual goals that match or stretch their capabilities and support your team's purpose.

☐ Clarify roles for your team members that will support the achievement of those goals.

☐ Support your team in learning from its experiences and celebrating its successes.

#### Drive for Results

☐ Gain and sustain the commitment of team members and other stakeholders who can impact the success of your team.

☐ Establish and use an implementation plan with milestones and measures.

# Team Leadership— Burden or Opportunity?

A key question for you to consider is:

*Is this team leader role simply one more burden to take on, or is it a special opportunity to build your capability for accomplishing things that you, as a single individual, could not accomplish?*

**A New Level of Outcomes is Possible**

The shift from individual contributor to team leader invites you to take on a new level of leadership and a more collaborative style of contribution. New kinds of results are possible, if you are you ready to…

- Take on difficult problems and mobilize the combined expertise of a group to solve them.

- See your best ideas taken and shaped by the contribution of other team members into robust solutions that make a difference.

- Break down walls of resistance and get people to cooperate and work together.

- Move a work unit to high levels of performance that give them a whole new sense of pride and identity.

- Mold your team members into a group who are as strongly committed to supporting each other as they are to accomplishing their personal goals.

Behind each of these types of outcomes is a leader who guides the team to success by directing and facilitating its collaborative performance. If you can imagine getting these results for yourself and your organization, then you will find this guide a rich resource.

# Tools You Will Find in This Guide

We invite you on an exciting learning journey as you take on the challenge of becoming an effective team leader. In the following pages you will find:

- An overall framework for Team Leadership that outlines your key roles and primary responsibilities and tools.

- A practical and proven model of team performance that will help you understand team behavior, diagnose team issues and identify appropriate choices for addressing those issues.

- A compendium of best practices that can readily become your "play book" of options for leading your team.

- A set of success strategies that organize these best practices into "game plans" for addressing the most frequent team leader challenges.

- A step-by-step process for creating a practical development plan for building your team leader skills.

To help you find relevant sections, the guide is organized around a Team Leadership Framework, illustrated on the next two pages. Take a few minutes to familiarize yourself with it as a big-picture orientation to this work. Note also the Quick Map, on the inside of the back cover. This flow chart illustrates the resources provided in this guide and the paths you might take in accessing them. Also take special note of the flow charts beginning on page 158. These flow charts diagram the 12 Success Strategies on which successful teams thrive. They provide you with handy process prescriptions for leading your team through most of the critical stages on the way to high performance.

Best wishes for a fruitful learning journey!

# Team Leadership Framework

Imagine the stream of activities you have to manage as a team leader. Next imagine four responsibilities that surround this flow of activity regardless of your type of team or chosen style of leadership. They operate together as a system, and the strategies and practices you choose for each will greatly shape your team's performance. They are presented visually here, and then described in more depth in the following pages. Whether you are a new team leader or a seasoned one, this Team Leader Framework can be a reminder of what you have to pay attention to in this role.

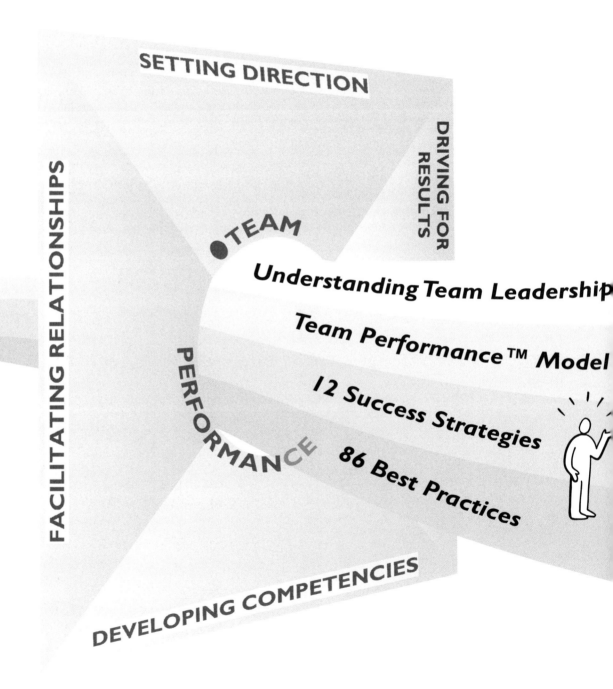

## How This Guide Is Organized

The main tools in this guide are illustrated below within the streams of activity you will have to manage. Early on is information about your role as a team leader and material that helps you think about it, as well as other orientation material. In the back of the book is specific help in creating a self-managed leadership development plan.

Next in the guide is a review of the Drexler/Sibbet Team Performance Model, drawn from more extensive information noted in this section. This provides a map to the repeating challenges the team will face, and that you will need to respond to as team leader. For meeting these particular challenges, we have outlined 12 success strategies that experienced team leaders use, one for the first and last stages of team performance and two strategies each for the other stages. Strategies are collections of practices that will help you and your team handle predictable phases of teamwork. The last section contains 80-plus page-at-a-glance best practices, organized within the stages of Team Performance.

### Team Leadership Roles
- Team Leader Self-Assessment
- Team Leader Roles & Types of Teams
- Team Leader Development Plan
- Leadership Styles Continuum

### Team Model
- Performance-Focused Framework
- Process Theory and Underlying Research
- Helpful Graphic Format
- Team Diagnostic Referenced to Best Practices

### Success Strategies
- From Team Formation through Action Learning
- Flow charts for Easy Reference
- Linked to Team Model & Best Practices
- Address Frequently Recurring Challenges

### Best Practices
- 86 Tested Best Practices for Teams
- Linked to Team Model & Strategies
- Presented in Page-at-a-Glance Format
- Supported by Interactive Graphic Templates

## Four Roles of Team Leadership

The visualization of the four roles of team leadership reflects the deeper structure of your job as a team leader. The vertical axis, *Setting Direction* and *Developing Competencies,* is future-focused. *Setting Direction* is literally your "uppermost" task, and should remain so at all times. *Developing Competencies* is a supporting role that anticipates the future needs of your team and the desire of team members to develop their abilities. The horizontal axis shows dimensions critical to managing the current stream of work. *Facilitating Relationships* is people oriented, and builds the connections required to support *Driving for Results,* which is more task focused. Your challenge is to engage effectively in each of these roles and weave them into an integrated leadership style.

# ROLES CHECKLIST

## Setting Direction

Your most critical role as a team leader is making sure your team has a clear sense of direction, where all members understand and fully support your team's purpose. This requires establishing…

☐ A Focused and Compelling Purpose—At the highest level the team's purpose needs to be so clear that members can readily separate the vital interests of the team from potential distractions. It should also be compelling enough to the team members that they are willing to support it fully.

☐ Vertical & Horizontal Goal Alignment—For your team to succeed it must make sure that its work aligns with the goals of the organization at large and those of any key stakeholders whose support is needed or who will be strongly impacted. Gaining this alignment is also part of direction setting.

☐ Clear Team and Individual Goals—The team's purpose needs to be translated into specific goals and priorities with targeted outcomes. This provides the traction needed to move to action. Individuals need to translate the team goals into personal goals as well.

Achieving agreement on direction requires that you provide the leadership to sort through any issues and questions that stand in the way. See *When to Go for Full Collaboration* on page 37 for guidelines on choosing the most appropriate style for achieving this.

## Facilitating Relationships

A team whose members strongly support each other can thrive even in adverse conditions. On the other hand, poor relationships among team members can undercut a team's effectiveness. The core elements you need to cultivate for your team to succeed are:

☐ Mutual trust and respect

☐ Open and effective communications

☐ Shared accountability for results

☐ Productive patterns of collaboration

## Developing Know-how

Your team has been brought together because members have the range of skills and knowledge needed to accomplish your team's goals. But there may be gaps. As leader you want to be sure your team has all the capabilities it will need. In both assembling and developing the capabilities of your team you will want to focus on:

☐ Requisite knowledge and skills

☐ Collaborative orientation to team work

☐ High personal standards of performance

## Driving for Results

Even with clear goals and all the capability you need, a team can fail in execution. You need shared processes for planning, organizing, performing and tracking your work, and attention paid to continuously adapting these processes to your specific type of team and work. Ideally, while others are actually doing the work, you are providing accountability and feedback on progress. The more your team shares in owning their processes, the easier your job is and the higher the performance of the team. The Success Strategies and Best Practices in this guide are rich resources for this job. You may need to adapt them to the type of team you are leading so you get results, whether you are a…

☐ Leadership or Implementation Team

☐ Temporary or Ongoing Team

☐ Collocated or Dispersed Team

☐ Single-Unit or Cross-Boundary Team

☐ Same-Culture or Culturally Diverse Team

*(See the following section on Types of Teams for a description of these critical differences and how they affect you as team leader).*

# Is Your Group a Team?

### Definition of a Team

A team is a group of people who must cooperate with each other in order to accomplish their objectives. Teams share:

- A purpose for working together

- A need for each other's abilities and commitment

- Accountability for results

Determining whether or not your group is really a team is a first step along the path to improving performance.

### Interdependent Tasks are Handled Best by Teams

We have already looked at how the growing complexity of work demands that people pool their knowledge and skills as a team to accomplish challenging tasks that the same persons working separately simply could not perform. In fact the word "team" implies a high level of interdependence.

It is obvious that a surgical team is highly interdependent. A surgeon cannot perform an operation successfully without complete coordination with the nurses and anesthesiologist. Similarly, a sales team for a highly technical system that

must be customized to each customer's unique needs requires a range of skills and knowledge that must be carefully coordinated.

It is that very issue of high interdependence which makes it essential that the team invest sufficiently in its own development, so that it is able to perform as an integrated whole.

### Some Teams Are Really Workgroups

However, before you make a big investment in your team's development, consider for a moment whether it is really a team. The level of interdependence isn't nearly so great for some groups that call themselves teams. A track team, for example, does not have nearly the same degree of interdependence as a soccer team. And many work "teams" are fully capable of performing their separate tasks with a minimum of interaction. So ask yourself, "How critical is each member to the overall success of the group?" If the answer is, "Members are each separately responsible for their fair share," then you probably aren't a strongly interdependent team. However, if you conclude that the loss of any member's contribution could undercut the whole effort, then you are definitely a team. This distinction is important because it tells you whether to focus substantial energy in building the team's clarity and commitment to its purpose and goals.

### Don't Underestimate the Degree of Interdependence

Many tasks appear on the surface to be independent of each other. In fact, we intentionally design work to be modular so that each component can proceed independently, knowing that it will fit into a larger framework as long as it conforms to prescribed standards. The danger in this kind of task segmentation is that the potential synergies and opportunities to leverage knowledge and capabilities are lost. An important role of the team leader is to assess where the real interdependencies lie and to ensure that the team works together on these elements of their work.

## YOUR GROUP IS A TEAM IF...

### It has high levels of interdependence

☐ The successful completion of its goals will require a synthesis of knowledge and skills that no single person possesses.

☐ The core of its work cannot be broken down into independent components, but requires that everyone work together.

☐ Team members believe that working cooperatively will lead to better results than working separately.

☐ Members belong to separate organizational units that need to work on a common task, the success of which will impact each of their units.

☐ There is an opportunity to provide your customers or constituents an integrated "solution" if different units can work together.

☐ There is a shared accountability for results (as with management teams).

☐ You have a mutual competitor you hope to out-perform and can gain advantage by pooling your efforts.

### Learning is a critical element for success

☐ The task or assignment requires a new or untested approach.

☐ Creativity and learning-by-doing are fundamental aspects of this task or assignment and can be encouraged, supported and enriched by group interaction.

☐ There is an overarching goal or opportunity that needs to take precedence over individual priorities.

### It needs to respond flexibly to changing conditions

☐ Its work is sufficiently variable in volume or difficulty that teamwork can improve both quality and productivity. (Self-managing teams with clearly defined accountabilities have repeatedly demonstrated their ability to take on and manage their work to high standards.)

☐ Its level of effort will need to be increased over the course of your project, and team members could assist in taking on, indoctrinating and integrating new members into the work.

☐ It needs to be able to mobilize for action on short notice.

*On the following page is an activity that you can conduct with your team to determine which tasks require real interdependence. Leading your group through this exercise will build commitment to whatever investment you choose to make in team development. Most people don't want their time to be wasted, and neither do you—so keep your efforts focused on those areas where you need real cooperation.*

## Identify How Much Actual Teamwork is Needed

Most groups have certain tasks that require cooperation. Having everyone be clear about where they need to work together and where they don't sets the stage for engaging your team around improving performance. The following activity will help you lead a discussion that accomplishes this. When everyone agrees on the core tasks that require cooperation, these become a baseline for teamwork, and can serve as the focus of your leadership efforts.

**What Kinds of Tasks Require Interdependence?**
The chart below illustrates some general types of teams and the kinds of tasks they might under-

take. Imagine writing down all the tasks your team is facing on sticky notes and arranging them on a similar chart. The tasks placed on the far right require full cooperation to complete. For tasks toward the left, members can work independently. Many tasks, of course, will require some of both and fall in the middle.

Interdependence is simply another word for "needing to cooperate." When you define this for your team, define "high interdependence," or a #10 on the scale, as that condition where you absolutely cannot complete a task without helping each other. If your team has lots of these kinds of tasks, you will benefit from investing strongly in team development. Low interdependence might mean you should focus on individual effectiveness rather than team effectiveness.

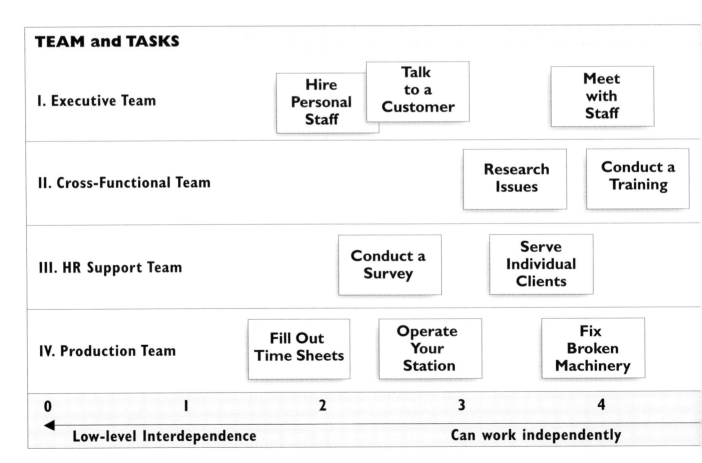

## Check Interdependence

**①** Get your team to agree to spend some time checking their need for teamwork.

**②** Pass out sticky notes and write down all tasks, one per note.

**③** Create a scale of interdependence on a white board or large plotter paper, from 1 to 10 as illustrated below.

**④** Ask your team members to intuitively post the sticky notes on the scale.

**⑤** Discuss what the card placements show about your level of team interdependence.

**⑥** Agree on the top items that require cooperation.

*Check if your team tasks require interdependence. Do not insist on "team work" unless you need it.*

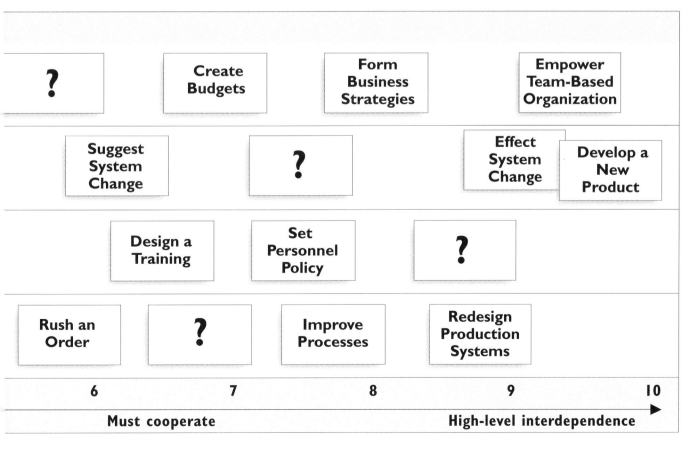

# What Type of Team Are You Leading?

## *Different Teams Require Different Responses*

Now that you have established if you are a team and how interdependent you are, it's important to look at what type of team you are leading. Your four team leader roles—*Setting Direction, Facilitating Relationships, Developing Competencies,* and *Driving for Results*—will apply to whatever type of team you are, but the strategies and practices you use will change depending on this next assessment. Take some time to step back, review the following checklists, and reflect on the type of team you are leading. This perspective will help you make better choices of which practices to propose to improve performance.

### Teams Have Multiple Differences

Many different kinds of task-oriented groups are called teams. They differ in structure, purpose, context and duration. They don't all have the clear focus and sets of rules that guide sports teams, for instance. These differences can be significant for you as team leader. Here are five of the most critical to think about now. Your team will fall on one side or the other of each of these dimensions:

| Less Complex | More Complex |
|---|---|
| • Implementation Teams | • Leadership Teams |
| • Ongoing Teams | • Temporary Teams |
| • Collocated Teams | • Dispersed Teams |
| • Single-Unit Teams | • Cross-Boundary Teams |
| • Same-Culture Teams | • Culturally Diverse Teams |

The most straightforward types of teams are the ones represented on the left-hand side of this list.

The right-hand ones are more complex, and are more challenging to lead.

Read over the descriptions of each team type and those that apply to your team. Look carefully at the corresponding list of tips and suggestions. Keep these in mind as you explore strategies and practices provided in this guide to help your specific type of team.

# Implementation or Leadership Teams

*Implementation teams* are those responsible for actually doing work and delivering the results desired by leadership. The team's autonomy may vary from having a very general assignment to having very specific instructions on both what to do and how to do it. Greater autonomy will mean you and your team will need to take more initiative.

You may be designated as the team leader or your team may be self-managed with shared leadership responsibilities. As organizations move to flatten their structure and reduce the number of supervisors, they are discovering that many teams are capable of self-management and take pride in their accomplishments and ability to handle challenges. If you are working in a more self-managed mode, your role will be more that of a facilitator than a team leader.

*Leadership teams* are responsible for guiding other people's work. They are accountable for setting the mission and vision of their organization and keeping it renewed, as well as maintaining a big-picture view of how different units fit into the larger organization and industry. In addition, they define and update strategies, ensure that adequate goals and plans are in place, monitor progress, and make required course corrections.

Leadership teams are also responsible for building organization capacity—modeling the desired values and behaviors, developing managers, resourcing staff, material and information, approving budgets, as well as establishing necessary organizational structures and processes. A leadership team's primary perspective and responsibility should be for the whole organization, in spite of the separate responsibilities of its members.

---

### Tips for Leading IMPLEMENTATION TEAMS

☐ Know your team's mandate, accountabilities and limits of autonomy and communicate them to your team.

☐ Ensure that individual goals align with your team's overall mandate and the organization at large.

☐ Identify the highly interdependent aspects of the team's work and establish clear processes and practices that support that work.

☐ Look for ways to continually develop the capabilities of your team.

☐ Regularly acknowledge good performance.

☐ Determine how you or your team will address patterns of inadequate performance by a team member.

☐ Be clear about how you are assessing team and individual performance.

---

### Tips for Leading LEADERSHIP TEAMS

☐ Advocate that the team develop a clear overall vision and direction.

☐ Ensure that members understand the difference between their role as a team member and their role as the leader of their own group.

☐ Clarify where members are free to act independently and where they need to work together interdependently.

☐ Clarify how decisions will be made.

☐ Establish constructive ways for members to share differences of opinion.

☐ Establish clear processes by which the team delegates, monitors, supports and holds accountable those to whom it has delegated goals and responsibilities.

☐ Be clear about what it means to fulfill/not fulfill a commitment made to the team.

☐ Clarify how the team will address not only the performance of the organization but also the vitality of its culture.

---

# *Ongoing* or *Temporary Teams*

*Ongoing teams* fulfill a set of functions or responsibilities that continue indefinitely. They can be either implementation or leadership teams. They are usually created to perform tasks that individuals cannot perform as effectively. An ongoing team is expected to organize itself for optimal use of its resources. The size of the team may fluctuate based on the workload, expanding around a core of experience and expertise.

*Temporary teams* are created to respond flexibly to emerging challenges without restructuring the organization. Temporary teams can be quickly assembled with the right mix of capabilities to handle a new initiative and then dissolved when the action has been accomplished. Members may be drawn from all relevant parts of the organization without changing basic organizational structures. With clear mandates and strong sponsors, a temporary team can mobilize quickly to address new opportunities and challenges.

## Tips for Leading **ONGOING TEAMS**

- [ ] Clarify whether your team's goals are aligned with the organization at large.

- [ ] Ask—"How has our purpose changed since we last explored it?"

- [ ] Identify any team tasks or activities that no longer serve a valuable purpose in the organization.

- [ ] Address any unresolved issues that have been allowed to shape the way the team works together. Ask—"What is this costing us in both performance and the well-being of the team?"

- [ ] Lead an exploration of potential opportunities that could help the team be more effective or grow beyond its current status quo.

## Tips for Leading **TEMPORARY TEAMS**

- [ ] Be sure the team's mandate or charter is clear.

- [ ] Clarify who the sponsor is and to whom the team is accountable.

- [ ] Address how the team's resource needs will be met.

- [ ] Invest time in team building and creating some shared best practices.

- [ ] Clarify how the team's success will be measured and how you will know when your work is done.

- [ ] Identify and address any competing priorities that team members face.

- [ ] Pay attention to any team members who have been forced onto the team, addressing any issues this creates and looking for ways to align their interests with those of the team.

- [ ] Establish processes for keeping major stakeholders involved and informed.

# Single-Unit or Cross-Boundary Teams

*Single-unit teams* are based in one organization and report to a single manager or point of control. Members share the same organizational affiliation, and are generally clear about their accountability.

---

### Tips for Leading SINGLE-UNIT TEAMS

☐ Make sure your work is aligned with your manager's expectations and goals.

☐ Clarify your authority as a team leader, and encourage the larger organization to deal with you regarding team transactions.

☐ Pay attention to the interfaces your team has with other parts of the organization.

---

*Cross-boundary teams* have members who report to different units of the organization, or even to other organizations. Members have different loyalties and present a greater challenge for leadership. This type of team is becoming increasingly common as organizations seek the advantage of complete solutions for their customers and constituents, and recognize the value of bringing together many different perspectives and interests to address complex needs.

If you are leading a cross-boundary team, you will need to balance the priorities of your team with the priorities placed on your members by their own units. Resource requirements for a cross-boundary team can become a source of contention if they are in competition with other units. Your work as a cross-boundary team, whether it be creating recommendations or producing a direct work product, will typically need to be accepted by the relevant operating units to become useful.

Since many cross-boundary teams are distributed over a number of locations and composed of members from a number of distinct cultures, you should look carefully at the subsequent tips relating to culture and location.

---

### Tips for Leading CROSS-BOUNDARY TEAMS

☐ Ensure that your team has a clear charter and that the charter is supported by all the participating units.

☐ Use the charter to clarify understandings regarding resource allocations and team member priorities.

☐ Actively promote sponsorship by someone who is senior enough to be able to resolve priority and resource issues that arise.

☐ Pay special attention during the startup phase to getting team member buy-in to the team's purpose, establishing a high level of trust among team members, and dealing explicitly with any issues of conflicting priorities.

☐ Establish communication protocols for keeping all relevant stakeholders appropriately informed during the life of the project. This includes making clear choices about groupware platforms and expectations for use.

☐ Clarify team member accountabilities, especially where members are responsible for gaining the support of their own groups.

☐ Anticipate the likely challenges of getting the team's output accepted and utilized. Establish an explicit strategy for managing the transition and transfer of ownership.

---

# Collocated *or* Dispersed Teams

*Collocated team* members are all together at the same physical location. This has some advantages in ready access to face-to-face meetings, support for informal work cultures and communities of practice, frequent opportunities for feedback, sharing common infrastructure, situational decision making, and greater ease in spotting problems that arise.

---

### Tips for Leading COLLOCATED TEAMS

☐ **Use the ease of contact to sustain informal relationships and regular acknowledgement of progress and problems.**

☐ **Set whatever explicit boundaries you need to get work accomplished, but remain accessible.**

☐ **Seek ways the team can learn about customers, other parts of the organization, and other stakeholders beyond those reached in informal daily contact.**

---

*Dispersed team* members are located at various physical locations sufficiently distant from each other that meeting at a common site is problematic. Here are some of the complications you may be facing if your team is dispersed:

- Face-to-face meetings are more costly in terms of money, time and stress and usually can't be held as frequently.

- Team members may have little prior history of working together.

- There is little opportunity for informal social reinforcement of relationships, or for feedback.

- Time zone differences make it difficult to connect during normal hours of work.

- Team members represent a variety of work and social cultures and may not realize or appreciate critical differences.

- Technical and administrative support infrastructures may not be available to all members.

- Supervising will require a lot of travel, a lot of trust and proactive communicating.

- Ad hoc decision-making processes that work face-to-face can prove to be confusing when interacting at a distance.

- Conflict between team members tends to get buried or erupt destructively.

- Gaining full organizational support often requires working through a multitude of channels simultaneously.

Taken together, these factors suggest that as a leader of a dispersed team you cannot rely on addressing the issues as they arise over the course of your project. You must instead set up clear and explicit processes to guide and structure your team's interactions and work, and invest the time to put them in place.

In the following list of tips, we used the Team Performance Model (TPM) to provide you with some general guidelines for leading dispersed teams, organized around the generic challenges all teams face. There is a more thorough description of this model and its stages on pages 22–35. The best practices are also organized around the stages of team performance as described in the TPM.

## Tips for Leading DISPERSED TEAMS

### 1. For Orientation

- ☐ Be explicit about your team's purpose and goals—put things in writing.
- ☐ Explain how the purpose aligns with your organization's goals.
- ☐ Employ a clear startup process with explicit norms and protocols.

### 2. For Trust Building

- ☐ Hold periodic face-to-face meetings if possible and concentrate on relationship building and mutual understanding—help team members to connect as people.
- ☐ Establish dependable, consistent communications. Use e-rooms and web conferencing if available.
- ☐ Provide explicit opportunities for members to raise reservations and concerns.
- ☐ Reach team agreement on communication protocols, including formats, availability, synchronous meetings and response times.

### 3. For Goal Clarification

- ☐ Be clear with members about the specific objectives of the team and the assumptions lying behind those objectives.
- ☐ Identify clearly who has responsibility for each of the team goals.
- ☐ Provide clear opportunities for team members to align their individual goals with the team's overall purpose and objectives.
- ☐ Provide any background material that team members should understand.

### 4. For Commitment to a Direction

- ☐ Capture all team and member commitments in clear documentation that remains easily accessible to all members.
- ☐ Be explicit about time and resource constraints.

- ☐ Explain how decisions will be made, or collectively agree on the process.
- ☐ Identify stakeholder support required and steps needed to secure it.

### 5. For Implementation

- ☐ Employ planning, scheduling and other groupware tools that support collaboration at a distance.
- ☐ Determine a process for regular updates and progress report teleconferences or web meetings.
- ☐ Target an early accomplishment that can reinforce patterns of success.
- ☐ Use any early difficulties as a chance to review the team's rules of engagement.

### 6. For High Performance

- ☐ Actively acknowledge successes and productive behavior, through regular communication.
- ☐ Help the relevant stakeholders in each member's local work community understand what is being achieved.
- ☐ Use established linkages to provide direct access to help for any member who needs assistance.
- ☐ Proactively communicate about changes and problems to head off rumors.

### 7. For Renewal

- ☐ Stage celebratory gatherings or teleconferences that acknowledge accomplishments and reflect on what was learned.
- ☐ Ensure that member contributions are captured in relevant repositories of organizational memory (letter to boss, article in group newsletter/website, etc.).
- ☐ Balance your own travel and work schedule to provide a healthy model for others.

# *Same-Culture* or *Culturally Diverse Teams*

Culture is that collective set of assumptions and expectations we use to make sense of the world and guide our behaviors—most of which have become such a natural part of our lives that we neither question them nor even consciously consider them. That is the reason culturally diverse teams are challenging.

*Same-culture teams* are easier to lead if you are from that same culture, since you are more likely to know the appropriate language, nuances, and style. They can, however, get blindsided if the team needs to deal with customers or other parts of the organization that have different cultures.

---

### Tips for Leading **SAME-CULTURE TEAMS**

☐ Work to identify where your team might be blindsided by all thinking the same way.

☐ Introduce experiences and people that will exercise your team's ability to think beyond its specific ways of working.

☐ Personally engage in experiences that provide you with a broader perspective.

---

*Culturally Diverse teams* have many advantages, but are also more challenging to lead. They are being encouraged because global and market-spanning organizations need the contributions of members from many parts of the organization and many parts of the globe. Diverse teams have the advantage of broader expertise. And this comes with the added complexity of different assumptions about how to work together. Because these assumptions are largely unconscious, you and your team members probably won't be able to readily identify the differences until you crash into your own ignorance. This makes your role as team leader particularly important in helping team members develop explicit agreements and practices for working together that will support meeting these challenges when they arise. The practices in this guide should help in that process.

---

### Traps to avoid with **CULTURALLY DIVERSE TEAMS**

☐ Using idioms of speech that are not understood outside the culture where they are used (for example, "We need to be prepared to go to the mat on this issue." "This option seems like a slam dunk." etc.)

☐ Praising and criticizing individual team members in a manner that is unacceptable in their culture (for instance, singling out an individual in some Asian cultures.)

☐ Disclosing controversial opinions and difficult feelings to team members in a manner that is unacceptable in their culture.

☐ Using language that is considered offensive.

☐ Assuming that team members hold the same values regarding consensus-based or hierarchical processes.

☐ Assuming that team members hold the same values regarding use of time (for example, task efficiency versus relationship building; prompt starts and ends to meetings versus respecting the natural flow of exchanges; rapid move-to-action versus thoughtful deliberation).

☐ Assuming that team members hold the same values regarding the use of humor and what is really funny.

☐ Failing to recognize others' points of pride or embarrassment that are culturally based.

---

## Tips for Leading CULTURALLY DIVERSE TEAMS

☐ When the team is being formed, ask members to share in detail about their best team experiences, and what made them special. Pay attention to what works for them in their particular cultures.

☐ Be more explicit than usual in getting everyone to say how they can work together across the stages of team performance. Cover goal setting, role clarification, decision-making, progress tracking, personal feedback, problem solving, learning reviews, acknowledgements and celebrations. Don't make assumptions that everyone will think the same way you do about these common team challenges.

☐ Use visual tools to engage members as a complement to speaking a common language, like English. The graphics will serve some of the same purpose translators do, illustrating another way to understand the material being discussed.

☐ Use low-risk get-acquainted processes that build relationships and mutual trust early in the life of the team, especially with people who come from high-context cultures and expect to know a lot of personal things about colleagues.

☐ Conduct frequent check-ins, perhaps using a brief period at the beginning of each team exchange as an opportunity for team members to catch up with each other. Keep it light and engaging.

☐ Encourage all members to actively ask for clarification of anything that isn't clear to them—especially in remote conferences. This is essential when there are language challenges. Give positive support to anyone who does this, especially in the early stages of the team's development.

☐ Model open feedback by inviting other team members to give you specific feedback on your own leadership approach and style. Go out of your way to demonstrate your willingness to use the feedback constructively.

☐ Be especially clear about all standards and expectations to which you intend to hold team members. Check carefully to ensure these are understood, or you may get very different results than you seek.

☐ Invest in a special face-to-face team building experience that will let people learn more about each other as individuals. This will greatly improve any remote communications.

☐ Instead of creating a "my way or your way" tension between persons of different cultures, encourage everyone to coinvent a "third way" that works for the team.

# The Drexler/Sibbet Team Performance™ Model

## *Moving into the River of Action*

If you've been reading through this guide sequentially, you will have thought through your role as a team leader, whether or not you are leading a true team, and what type of team you are leading. But how does all this come together in action?

The illustration below shows the graphic river that has been running through this guide, symbolizing the ongoing work and activity surrounding your team. In it are some of the bigger challenges you may well face, such as:

- Team Formation
- Goal Alignment
- Project Planning
- Decision Making
- Progress Reviews
- Creative Problem Solving
- Action Learning

Constraining one side of the river of action are your high hopes. The other bank is the real world of operational and physical constraints.

### Learning a Model for Team Performance

Over many years of working with teams, Allan Drexler and David Sibbet came to appreciate that these types of team challenges are somewhat predictable, and arise from repeating sets of concerns that all teams face during the stages of their work. The following pages of this guide review the Drexler/Sibbet Team Performance Model (TPM) they developed during more than 10 years of collaboration. It is a combination of extensive research on teams by Jack Gibb, several decades of field experience by Allan and David, and a general theory of process articulated by Arthur M. Young in the 1970s. The model

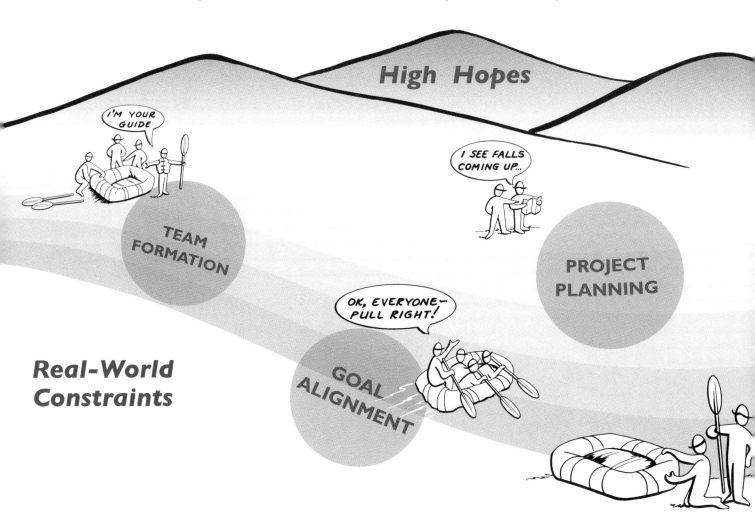

illustrates the recurring challenges teams face, and the indicators that tell you if a team has successfully addressed them. It has become one of the most robust frameworks for understanding team dynamics.

**Best Practices Are Responses to a Team's Generic Challenges**

What is not common to all teams is how you as a leader respond to these challenges. This is the area of best practice, and has grown steadily over the years since the Drexler/Sibbet Team Performance Model was first developed. It is a job you will need to take on personally as you develop your own repertoire. In Section II, we have included 86 different practices to help you begin that process.

In Section III, you will find flow charts, called Success Strategies, for guiding your team through 12 of the most typical team challenges. These Success Strategies weave together relevant practices from Section II into integrated processes.

**Begin with Understanding the Model**

The best way to jump into the river of action is to begin to imagine it from the team's point of view. Think of your team as though it were a group on a rafting trip. You would most certainly benefit from a map of the river that showed you where the waterfalls and major rapids were. That is what the TPM will provide. The following pages provide an introduction, and then strategies for implementation.

Drexler/Sibbet

# Team Performance™ model

**I.**
**Orientation**
*WHY*
*am I here?*

*Resolved*
• Purpose
• Team Identity
• Membership

*Unresolved*
• Disorientation
• Uncertainty
• Fear

*Resolved*
• Mutual regard
• Forthrightness
• Reliability

**2.**
**Trust Building**
*WHO*
*are you?*

*Unresolved*
• Caution
• Mistrust
• Facade

*Resolved*
• Explicit assumptions
• Clear, integrated goals
• Shared vision

**3.**
**Goal Clarification**
*WHAT*
*are we doing?*

*Resolved*
• Assigned roles
• Allocated resources
• Decisions made

*Unresolved*
• Apathy
• Skepticism
• Irrelevant competition

*Unresolved*
• Dependence
• Resistance

**4.**
**Commit-ment**
*HOW*
*are you?*

## CREATING

| 1. Orientation | 2. Trust Building | 3. Goal Clarification | 4. Commitment |
|---|---|---|---|
| When teams are forming everybody wonders *WHY* they are here, what their potential fit is and whether others will accept them. People need some kind of answer to continue. | Next, people want to know *WHO* they will work with—their expectations, agendas and competencies. Sharing builds trust and a free exchange among team members. | The more concrete work of the team begins with clarity about team goals, basic assumptions and vision. Terms and definitions come to the fore. WHAT are the priorities? | At some point discussion need to end and decision must be made about *HO* resources, time, staff—all the bottom-line constraints—will be managed Agreed roles are key. |

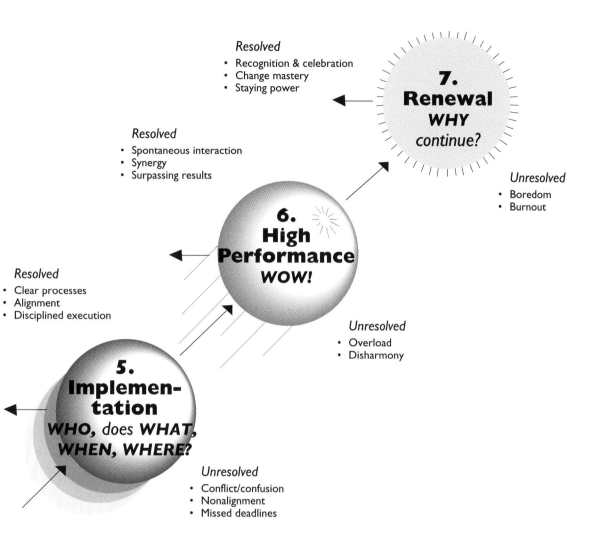

*Resolved*
- Recognition & celebration
- Change mastery
- Staying power

**7.
Renewal
WHY
continue?**

*Resolved*
- Spontaneous interaction
- Synergy
- Surpassing results

*Unresolved*
- Boredom
- Burnout

**6.
High
Performance
WOW!**

*Resolved*
- Clear processes
- Alignment
- Disciplined execution

*Unresolved*
- Overload
- Disharmony

**5.
Implemen-
tation
WHO, does WHAT,
WHEN, WHERE?**

*Unresolved*
- Conflict/confusion
- Nonalignment
- Missed deadlines

# SUSTAINING

## Implementation
eams turn the corner
hen they begin to
·quence work and settle
1 *WHO* does *WHAT,*
*HEN,* and *WHERE* in
·tion. Timing and sched-
ing dominate this stage.

## 6. High Performance
When methods are mas-
tered, a team can begin to
change its goals and flexibly respond to the envi-
ronment. The team can
say, "WOW!" and surpass
expectations.

## 7. Renewal
Teams are dynamic.
People get tired; members
change. People wonder
"*WHY* continue?" It's time
to harvest learning and
prepare for a new cycle of
action.

## JACK GIBB'S RESEARCH ON GROUP PROCESS

The Drexler/Sibbet Team Performance™ Model integrates Jack R. Gibb's original research on group behavior with the process theories of Arthur M. Young (described on the next page).

Working in the 1940s and 1950s as one of the pioneers of applied behavior science, Gibb studied a large number of groups and discovered that people bring the following four basic concerns to all social interactions:

- the **acceptance concern,** which is related to the formation of trust, the acceptance of one-self and others, a decrease in anxiety, and an increase in confidence (this concern in part involves membership and degrees of membership on a team);

- **data concerns** about the flow of perceptions, feelings, and ideas through the team and the individual, and the social system for expressing them;

- the **concern for goal formation**—the process of team goal setting, problem solving,

and decision making——and the integration of the intrinsic motivations of individuals (goal setting in part involves productivity, having fun, creating, learning, and growing); and

- the **control concern** for mechanisms by which activities are regulated, coordinated, and put into a useful sequence.

In Gibb's scheme, these concerns remain throughout the life of a team. They cannot be completely resolved. The concerns are highly interdependent; success in dealing with one set of issues clearly affects the ability to deal with others. For example, when a team has not resolved basic membership issues, it can hardly have the kind of free flow of data that supports good decision making. In theory, the four primary categories of concerns are neat abstractions; in real life, they are messy and do not come compartmentalized, arranged in a fixed hierarchy or sequence. However we find them, they remain the fundamental themes that all teams must continually address. How they are resolved always affects how well a team works.

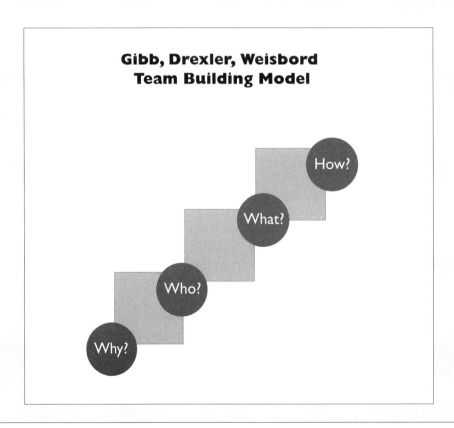

**Gibb, Drexler, Weisbord
Team Building Model**

# ARTHUR M. YOUNG'S THEORY OF PROCESS

Arthur M. Young was a physicist and mathematician interested in cosmology, or theories of explanation. He developed a comprehensive system for understanding the relationship between physical law and the human experience based on the discoveries of science itself.

Young set out in the early 1930s to develop a unified theory of how universal systems relate to each other, caught up in the general efforts of the early 20th century to describe a unified field theory integrating the major findings of science. In the process he spent a good number of years in the 1930s and '40s grounding his thinking in the practical process of inventing and developing the world's first commercially licensed helicopter, the Bell 47. He came out of this work and parallel research believing that the unity of things cannot be found by examining forms and structures and deterministic rules, but by appreciating the nature of process—the actions of the photon and fundamental particles upon which all else is based. He came to see that all process in the universe is playing out a creative tension between freedom and constraint, between the potential of the photons of light and the constraints of cause and effect at the molecular

level. When matter finds the combinatory rules at this level, it can then turn back toward freedom through the evolved structures of plants, animals and humans.

Young observed that all processes begin with some unexpressed potential that begins moving in some direction, eventually joining other forces until it achieves some identity, thereby creating the conditions for forms to combine into more complex arrangements. Mastering the rules of these arrangements then allows a turn toward freer and freer expression of the initial potential.

Applied to teams, this pattern confirms Gibb's research, and provided Allan and David a pattern for the sustaining stages of team development. It also helped them understand why the formative steps are so important and persistent throughout a team's life. Young's notion that freedom can be regained by mastering the initial constraints provides a conceptual template for understanding the conditions necessary for high performance. (For a detailed description of Arthur M. Young's Theory of Process, read Young's *The Reflexive Universe* (Delacourt Press, 1976), or go to www.arthuryoung.com.)

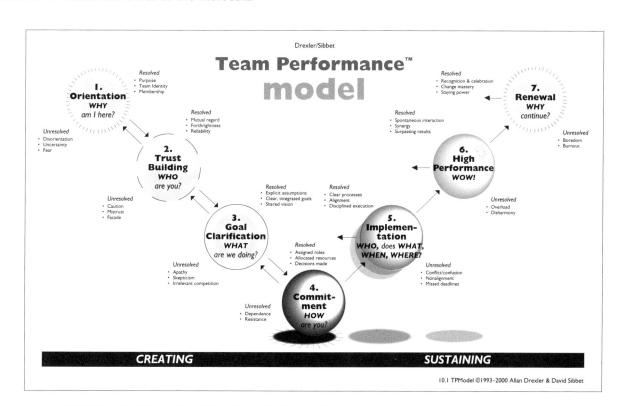

# Stage I:
# Orientation

## *Why Am I Here?*

Orientation is about team members assessing what it will mean to be a member of the team. They need to understand the reason the team exists, what will be expected of them and how they will benefit from membership. In a new team, these are individual concerns, for the group is only potentially a team. That is why they are illustrated as occurring in the imagination.

### Team Purpose

The key question for the Orientation stage is "Why am I here?" Part of the answer has to do with the team's purpose. A satisfactory answer would explain why the team exists and what is expected of it. This is why setting direction and clarifying charters is so central to team leadership. To the extent that members embrace that purpose, they begin to identify with the team. To the extent that the purpose is vague or at odds with what the members care about, they withhold their allegiance and feel disorientation, uncertainty and maybe even fear.

### Team Identity

Team members individually need to have a sense of identity in relation to the team, a conviction that they can make a difference to the team and

that the work of the team will make a difference for them. It's "Why am I here?" Resolving these issues allows people to feel that they fit into the team.

### Membership

Orientation also concerns the team as a whole. The focal question becomes, "Why are we here?" If team members know who they are as a team, what they stand for and what they are about, then they form a strong sense of themselves as one group. New participants will be concerned about whether or not they will be accepted as members in the group. Part of orientation in later stages of teamwork is making sure that this concern is handled so people can focus on the work.

As a team leader, taking responsibility for orientation at the beginning of a team's life, and sustaining attention to it throughout its work, is one of the primary jobs of a leader. It is what *setting direction* is all about.

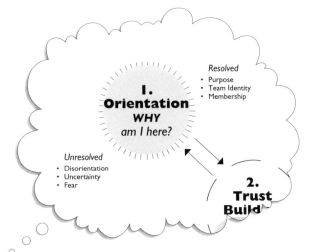

# Stage 2:
# Trust Building

## *Who Are You?*

Trust is a measure of one's willingness to depend on others for something that is important. Because team members have to depend on each other to be successful, trust is essential, in direct relation to how much interdependency exists. Initially trust involves some risk and uncertainty about dealing with strangers. This is why the key question is "Who are You?" An unstated aspect of this is wondering "What will you expect from me?" For a team to work well, members need to accept that they can depend on one another and that the results of getting involved are acceptable.

### Mutual Regard

For trust to sustain itself among team members, everyone needs to show him or herself to be worthy of that trust. Mutual regard is one of the results of having trust, and is built over time through knowledge and experience. As a fundamental element in team performance, trust persists as a concern, and grows stronger as it is revisited at each subsequent stage.

### Forthrightness

When trust is strong, information flows among team members. They are forthright with one another, willing to share their expertise and tell the truth as they see it. They have confidence in one another and in themselves, enough to air their views and come to grips with differences of opinion. When trust is low, team members are cautious and protective, and the open flow so necessary to effective teamwork is lost.

### Reliability

To trust other team members you also have to know enough about them to believe that they have the needed competency to fulfill their roles and that they are willing to act in the best interests of the team. This quality may not be assessable at first, but can surface as a trust issue during later implementation issues.

As a team leader, investing in trust building early pays off handsomely later on. It is especially important to pay attention to this set of concerns if your team is culturally diverse, dispersed, and cross boundary. Facilitating relationships is a lot about building trust among members. The higher the trust level among team members the less work there will be for you in handling relationship issues.

# Stage 3:
# Goal Clarification

## *What Are We Doing?*

Sometimes teams have precise charters that specify what they are responsible for accomplishing. More often, they are given a broad mandate and need to make choices about how they will pursue that mandate and translate it into goals. "What Are We Doing?" is a more immediate question than the larger question of purpose asked during Orientation.

### Explicit Assumptions

If your team is new, there is a lot of information that you must exchange to develop mutual understanding of the work involved. The activity testing task interdependency described on pages 12–13 is the kind of thing you would do during this stage to make assumptions about the work explicit.

### Clear Integrated Goals

Your central task in Stage 3 is to clarify what your team is to do, specifically. This means integrating the long-term goals expressed in your overall mission with short-term objectives concerning deliverables and immediate results you must produce. Objectives serve as progress markers that are as measurable or testable as possible. This phase also involves individuals setting their own goals in alignment with the team goals, especially if you are leading a workgroup where people work somewhat independently.

Without clear understanding and agreement regarding the team's goals, the team will not be able to perform effectively.

### Shared Vision

Implicit in high performance is the idea that team members are inspired to excel. Extensive research on sports performance shows that high performers can imagine success, and see it vividly. This is what it means to have a vision. As a team leader, if you can lead your group to articulate a real vision of what success looks like early in your process, your chances of reaching it are greater. A vision provides the focus and energy that bring objectives to life and bring meaning to hard work.

# Stage 4: Commitment

## *How Will We Do It?*

When goals are clear and options have been identified, the team is eager to act. The question now becomes, "How will we do it?" This stage occurs at the bottom of the "V" in the TPM, the point of greatest constraint, because making the choices implied by this question requires the team members to commit themselves to a specific course of action.

### Assigned Roles

A paramount concern of your team will be the specific roles and responsibilities each member will assume. Clarity and alignment includes agreements about functions, authorities and responsibilities. The role definitions have to be complete enough to cover all the tasks that must be done to accomplish the team's goals without creating overlaps and role conflicts. A big part of your job as team leader is to help match goals to competencies, and help people step into roles that will develop their abilities and improve results for the team.

### Allocated Resources

In addition to role clarity, your team must deal with another constraint—how to provide for and deploy its limited resources, including time and money. These hard choices usually involve setting aside some useful tasks because the resources are

not available to support them. Unclarity in this area breeds indecision and stalls work.

### Decisions Made

Finally, a team needs to get clear about how members will work together. How will decision-making authority be shared? How will members stay in touch with one another? Who can spend what funds? When a team has made these difficult decisions and set its course, it often feels a release of energy. Decisions begin to flow, and work begins to progress. This is what Young describes as a "turn"—in this case toward high performance.

The failure to resolve Stage 4 is typically expressed as a reluctance or even outright resistance by members to accept responsibility for the team's tasks, or simply deferring to the team leader in a dependent way.

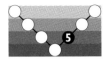

# Stage 5: Implementation

## Who Does What, When, Where?

The key question a team in implementation asks is "Who does what, when, and where?" The concern is the sequence of work. A clear schedule, strategy or process liberates the team to move into action confidently. Conflicts and confusion arise when there is commitment but no clear way forward.

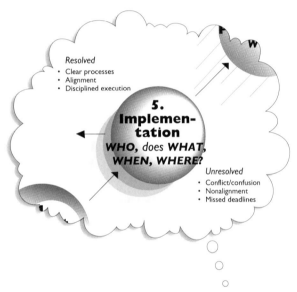

### Clear Processes

Confusion over how to accomplish work ties up a great deal of energy and attention on a team. As a team leader, one of your jobs is to *Drive for Results,* and helping to get process issues solved is a big part of the job. When the sequence of work is understood, people can devote themselves to the work itself. One of the challenges in cross-boundary and culturally diverse teams is agreeing on common processes.

### Alignment

It is not enough to have clear processes. They need to be aligned with the purpose and objectives you set earlier. Your job as team leader is now to reinforce the directions in which the team is moving. Sometimes the processes need to adapt, like a sailboat tacking in the wind.

### Disciplined Execution

The final challenge of Stage 5 is to integrate all related tasks into a smooth operation that delivers results, with sequence and timing coordinated, activities meshing and the whole system in balance. This is what disciplined execution means in practice. Parts must integrate with the whole if your team is to experience full benefit from everyone's individual contributions.

Successful implementation allows some freedom back into the process. Trial and error is essential when tackling work that is brand new. Some improvisation is usually necessary to stay on course even with understood work. It is important not to assign tasks and schedule their completion so rigidly that the work becomes too segmented. Meeting regularly for progress reviews and check-ins helps the team stay aligned and flexible. It is your team leader responsibility to keep sight of the overall purpose and ultimate objectives.

# Stage 6:
# High Performance

## *Wow!*

High performance is a "WOW" state, as a team masters its processes and begins to experience the ability to change goals as well as achieve them. You can feel it when it happens and observe its effects, but not necessarily control this possibility the same way you can earlier stages. It is a result of the team getting to that flow state where high trust guides the group competency. In a state of high performance, boundaries and individual limits are broken through, things move together, everything clicks, and everyone seems to respond as though they are part of a unified whole.

### Spontaneous Interaction

We all start out life as spontaneous, playful children. This capacity is still present for us as adults. When trust and acceptance of one another supports a lively give-and-take, and mutual knowledge of one another enables everyone to communicate clearly and efficiently and to anticipate one another's needs, then spontaneity emerges. High performing teams infuse their work with a unique spirit and creativity that sets them apart.

### Synergy

If your team achieves high performance, it will seem like something bigger is happening than anything that could be achieved from individual efforts. This is the synergy that comes when people bring out the best in one another, pushing beyond what any of them are able to accomplish individually. There may be conflicts, but these are readily engaged and resolved. Their work together takes on a fluidity that enables them to adapt and change as if in unison.

### Surpassing Results

The net effect is accomplishments that go beyond ordinary bounds and a collective experience on the part of the team that is a source of real pride and satisfaction. Several things can catalyze this move from implementation to high performance. A crisis may release bursts of cooperation and

energy that allow people to rise to an occasion. Or a team can experience a breakthrough in the context of working hard to crack problems and lay a foundation for high trust and high flexibility. In both cases the results can surpass expectations.

Much of the work of a team leader in a high performance team is to support and encourage, and keep from upsetting the balance and synergy. It is a fragile state, as the next stage suggests.

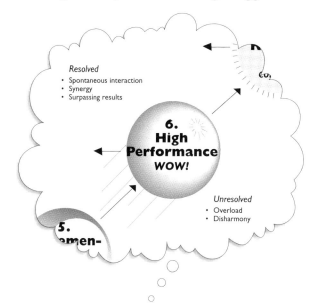

# Stage 7: Renewal

## Why Continue?

Over time the conditions that initially set your team in motion may change. High performance is demanding. Don't be surprised if people ask "Why continue?" This key question reminds us that team performance is an ongoing process, and must be renewed by returning to Stage 1 and reassessing if the work is still needed, worthwhile, and has some personal value and meaning.

*Resolved*
• Recognition & celebration
• Change mastery
• Staying power

**7. Renewal**
**WHY** continue?

*Unresolved*
• Boredom
• Burnout

**6.** 

Renewal practices put your team back in touch with the meaning the work has for them and renews their commitment to it. If the work is completed, renewal can be freeing, enabling members to move on to new challenges.

### Recognition and Celebration

Whether you are simply recharging to continue or are completing a process, acknowledging people's work and celebrating their contributions helps complete key cycles and allows everyone to move on with good feeling. Recognition is one of the strongest forces in creating great places to work, and in getting superior behavior from team members.

### Managing Change

In today's dynamic environment, most teams will benefit from addressing renewal questions regularly. This involves aligning the fit between what the team is doing and what individual members consider meaningful or important for their lives. It also involves integrating new people, and working out leadership transitions if there are promotions from all your good work.

### Staying Power

Renewal does not just happen at the end of a team's work together. In some sense teams are always in transition. Renewal also means examining what has been learned, so that it carries forward to the next challenge. Ideas, discoveries and new practices emerge out of team experiences that are worth preserving and sharing with others. In fact, it is the repeated cycling through all seven stages and staying conscious about what is being learned that builds the strong repertories of genuinely high performing work cultures.

# SOME TIPS FOR USING THE TEAM PERFORMANCE MODEL

### Don't view the stages as a fixed sequence

☐ Think of the stages as core elements of performance that repeat rather than as a defined pattern that needs to be followed in a lock-step sequence. Once a team is formed and working, all of these dynamics are active. They are ordered in the model left to right in terms of which is more fundamental, rather than by a chronological progression of when you deal with them. For example, a team may not fully grasp its purpose (stage 1) nor have a sufficient level of trust (stage 2) until it has first struggled with defining its goals (stage 3) and testing the commitment of its members to take on the challenge they face (stage 4). On the other hand, to fully resolve a stage's concerns you will need to have resolved the prior stages' concerns. People will not fully commit without some sense of purpose, trust and clarity. The arrows indicate that cycling back to address more fundamental concerns is a part of all teamwork. If you are having a problem at one stage, something unresolved in earlier stages is a good place to begin in finding out why.

### Resistance indicates an unresolved stage

☐ The first four stages are aimed at converging on a shared commitment regarding a specific course of action. Commitment is the key to regaining freedom of action through aligned, focused teamwork. But because the process is taking on greater constraint in the early stages, you can expect resistance as members recognize that they are also being asked to set aside other options. Some "storming" is inevitable. If concerns of early stages are ignored or glossed over, resistance will amplify. Gibb (page 26) contended people naturally move back toward the earlier stages if their concerns aren't addressed. If goals are ambiguous, for instance, people will wonder whom they are working with and wonder if leadership is to be trusted. Thus resistance is a good diagnostic signal for you to return to unattended stages and deal with those issues directly. As tempting as it is to push ahead through the turn of Stage 4, this will only increase the chance that the unaddressed

issue will make it impossible to implement or achieve anything like high performance.

### Use the model openly with your team

☐ The Team Performance Model was created to provide a common language for everyone on a team. It is not just a team leader tool. Teams that share clear road maps of where they are headed are better able to handle the changes in terrain they encounter, and to make your leadership job easier. Consider sharing the model with the team during the startup process and at any point where the team is bumping into unresolved issues or simply wants to tune up its process for working together.

### Any substantial change will require that your team step back and address prior stages

☐ None of the stages are ever ultimately resolved. The loss of a key resource, the imposition of a new requirement, a change in an important factor in the external environment—any of these can impact the team's purpose, the level of trust among its members, or the appropriateness of the current goals.

### High Performance (stage 6) is not an end state that, once achieved, needs only to be sustained

☐ It is instead a dynamic stage, very sensitive to changing conditions. It is more appropriate, in fact, to view bursts of high performance as the fruit of diligently addressing and resolving the issues of the prior stages.

### Mastering team performance ultimately lays the groundwork for your next cycle through the process

☐ You and others may move to new teams or start over with your old one. As team leader you play a vital role in supporting the growth of the team's competence beyond the achievement of specific performance goals. The Renewal Stage (stage 7), with its focus on learning, appreciation and incorporation of new success strategies and best practices, is easy to skip in the press of moving on. However, it is as vital as each of the prior stages in achieving team effectiveness and sustained high performance.

# Why Teams Fail

If teams have so many advantages, why do they so often fail to achieve the results they were created to accomplish? The TPM model provides a framework for appreciating some of the reasons they fail.

1. **Unclear purpose and goals:** Unclear priorities are probably the number one reason for team failure. This is why setting direction is so important in team leadership. Having too many goals can be as problematic as having unclear goals.

2. **Members don't trust leadership:** If you can't win the trust of your team, you are imposing an impediment that is very hard to overcome. Conversely, once trust is established, it tends to build and spread.

3. **Inadequate teaming skills:** Most of our training has prepared us to be individual contributors, not team players, and most organizations reinforce this individual focus by setting individual goals, measuring individual performance and rewarding individuals instead of teams. Teams fail when they can't:

   • Put team goals before personal agendas

   • Understand assumptions and seek to understand ideas and points of view different from their own

   • Include everyone with respect for their contributions

   • Address conflicts constructively

   • Invite feedback and constructive criticism

   • Recognize and celebrate others' successes

   • Continually seek ways to support and improve the quality of relationships

   • Seek to learn from mistakes and failures instead of blaming and defending

4. **Lack of stakeholder involvement and commitment:** Teams can forget they are part of a larger organization. Failure to gain the support of critical stakeholders and the organization at large can leave the results of a strong team effort ignored or marginalized, with performance undermined because there is no foundation of larger commitments to "bounce off of."

5. **Interpersonal dynamics and commitment are ignored in a rush to implementation:** Focusing on the work at hand and giving little attention to interpersonal dynamics and the fundamental commitment of team members means that small concerns grow into major issues.

6. **Leadership fails to trust team performance:** A barrier to high performance is over-control by leadership and failure to trust things like shared values, a compelling vision, and flexible processes. The very practices that initially allow teams to get some results can prevent greater results if freedom isn't reintroduced.

7. **No time is spent on renewal:** Burnout is widespread in organizations. Not only do people belong to many teams at once, few spend any time really learning from each other in a way that carries over to other work. People who are continually unrecognized do not perform well.

# When to Go for Full Collaboration

## A Collaboration Continuum for Team Leaders

The TPM model does not deal explicitly with the challenge of picking an appropriate style for leading your team. As you prepare to select success strategies and best practices to improve your team performance, consider where you are on the collaboration continuum.

### Do I Simply Take Charge?

As team leader you are continually faced with the challenge of determining when to take charge and simply tell your team what to do, and when to facilitate your team working through how to proceed on a collaborative basis.

If yours is a true team it exists because it brings together a collective capability no individual team member possesses. All the interdependent tasks involved in your work need to be performed collaboratively. However, it is also clear that it would be highly inefficient to conduct all of the team's business in a fully collaborative format. There are many tasks that are best performed by individuals or a few team members working independently.

### When Do I Collaborate?

You need to be able to assess whether a task requires a collaborative approach or is better handled as an independent assignment. (Often it is a combination of the two, properly sequenced—for example, the team collaboratively identifies the best approach to a complex problem. That approach includes a number of tasks, such as data gathering or analysis, that are best performed as independent assignments.)

Assessing these factors will help determine the best approach:

1. **Capability**—Do the persons undertaking the task have the needed skills and knowledge?

2. **Clarity**—Is there a clear objective and approach, and do the team members undertaking the task understand the desired outcomes and the intended approach?

3. **Alignment**—Is there full support among the team members and any other critical stakeholders for this approach?

4. **Motivation**—Are team members positive about undertaking this task?

Think of it as a continuum where the degree of collaboration that is appropriate is determined by the combined assessment of these four factors (see table below).

The leadership style most appropriate for full collaboration, *Involving,* is summarized in the chart on the following page. However, there are other leadership styles more appropriate when full collaboration is not needed. The chart describes three others, *Directing, Convincing* and *Supporting,* and the conditions for which they are appropriate.

The four leadership styles are listed in order from most directive to least directive.

### COLLABORATION CONTINUUM

| Team Leader Provides Direction | | Full Collaboration Needed |
|---|---|---|
| • Team members fully capable of task | *Capability* | • No one person has all the needed skills/knowledge |
| • Goal and approach identified and understood by team members | *Clarity* | • No clear goal and/or approach identified |
| • Team and critical stakeholders fully supportive | *Alignment* | • Team and critical stake-holders strongly disagree |
| • Team members positive about undertaking task | *Motivation* | • Team members resistant |

# TEAM LEADERSHIP STYLES

| Leadership Style | Task Complexity | Capability/ Willingness/ Alignment of Team |
|---|---|---|
| • *DIRECTING—* stating clearly what needs to be accomplished by whom and when | • If task is clear and unambiguous | • If performer(s) have the requisite skills, understand the rationale and support the task's achievement |
| • *CONVINCING—* providing a clear proposal and rationale, addressing concerns through explanation | • If task requires explanation, either how, why or both (clarification of priority, utility, methodology, etc.) | • If team members need help understanding how to proceed or are not convinced of the approach, but are open to persuasion |
| • *INVOLVING—* inviting team members to participate in formulating how best to proceed, with leader acting as facilitator | • If overall goal is unclear or there is no clear idea or agreement on how best to achieve it | • If no single person has the requisite skills. Lack of agreement on approach, resistance to ideas from others; |
| • *SUPPORTING—* leader facilitates constructive engagement but avoids taking responsibility for resolution | • If task is best resolved by team members themselves. They are closest to the problem, most affected by it and best able to resolve it | • If there are strong emotions around the issue, typically regarding significant interpersonal disagreements |

**DIRECTING** is the fundamental style of leadership. People expect a leader to take charge by stating clearly what needs to be done. As long as the leader has legitimate authority and credibility and the directive makes sense to team members, they will willingly comply. Note that leaders do not need to have their own solution in hand to effectively use this style. The style is equally effective for getting a team engaged in working together to find a solution (e.g.–"I want everyone to pitch in and work together on this problem"). Directing works well in the beginning stages of a new team that does not have any agreements yet.

If the proposal doesn't make sense, or is not well understood, or the leader is working to establish credibility, then he/she needs to use the **CONVINCING** style, offering a clear proposal, backing it up with a compelling rationale, and addressing concerns with appropriate explanations.

**INVOLVING,** the fundamental style for collaboration, consists of inviting others to participate in mutually determining the best way forward and providing an appropriate process by which they can contribute and participate. When using an involving style, the leader:

- clarifies the purpose and process

- invites and encourages full participation

- uses clarification statements and summaries to keep the process on track

- supports diversity of opinions to exchange full exploration of ideas

- tests for consensus

- checks for commitment

**SUPPORTING,** the least directive of the styles listed, is a valuable style for helping resolve issues that do not directly impact the work of the team while keeping the responsibility for resolution directly on the parties involved. The key to this style is to actively facilitate an appropriate process for achieving resolution of the issue but to avoid getting drawn into solving the issue yourself. You could think of it as a practical form of counseling or mediation. It is not an appropriate style for facilitating collaborative team efforts focused on achieving clear mandates for which you are responsible as team leader. It is, however, appropriate for self-managing teams or high performance teams that have a high degree of trust.

# Section II:

## Best Practices for Team Performance

- How to Use This Section

- For Orienting to Purpose

- For Trust Building

- For Clarifying Objectives

- For Committing to Direction
  and Roles

- For Implementing

- For High Performance

- For Renewal

- Using the Practices with
  Dispersed Teams

# How to Use This Section

## *Think of This Resource as Your Playbook for Best Team Practices*

Quarterbacks and point guards have a whole set of plays they can call depending on the specific situation they are facing. As leader of your team you can think of these practices as your available plays.

### Getting Started

Everything in team performance starts with what the team thinks its purpose and desired outcomes are. This is the information that will help you pick which best practice to use to move through the stages of team performance. This, of course, cannot be contained in a guidebook, but must be provided by you.

The next step is to search through the sections and find a best practice that you think you could

use that will meet your objectives. Try it out. Modify it to suit the unique qualities of your team. Make it your own.

### Play "What's Next?"

A leader benefits from getting the team to see the value in whatever it does, learn from its experience and focus on "what's next." Practices can be combined into a whole process to provide focus and build momentum. Your main challenge is to have choices to help your team successfully address each stage as it moves toward high performance. You won't need all the practices included here, but you'll need to master some basic ones for each stage.

### Many Practices Can Be Used Across the Different Stages

You will notice as you begin to use this book that the practices in the beginning are fundamental ones that you will continue to use again and again in later stages of team work. In general,

## Team Startup

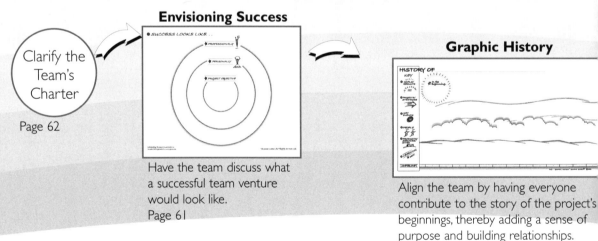

### MEETING 1

Clarify the Team's Charter
Page 62

**Envisioning Success**

Have the team discuss what a successful team venture would look like.
Page 61

**Graphic History**

Align the team by having everyone contribute to the story of the project's beginnings, thereby adding a sense of purpose and building relationships.
Page 70

the best practice is included in the stage of process when you would most likely first introduce it. You will soon discover that once you have experience with how a practice works, you can use it many other ways and places than are indicated here. You can combine and overlay them in very interesting ways, in addition to using them in their basic form. For instance, Trust Building practices can be used throughout the life of a team, as can the Clarification and Commitment practices.

### Working with Teams Online
Practices suitable for use online are marked with a **V** icon. At the end of this section are specific guidelines for using these practices with dispersed teams.

### Sample Process Flow
A typical team startup process is illustrated on this page, showing one sequence of best prac-

tices arranged one after the other to make a full process design. Each step is described, and indicates the page where you can find the Page-at-a-Glance practice in more detail.

### Use Sticky Notes for Design
If you have a team process you are planning, leaf through this book with a pad of sticky notes and record the names and pages of practices that look like they might be helpful. Then just play around with the sequence on a time-block agenda like the one included at the end of this introductory section. Organize it so that it seems right for you, then show it to someone else, talking them through the specific pages so that they can imagine what you have in mind.

### Worksheets
Pages 45 and 46 provide a sample time-block agenda and a blank practice template to support your working with this guide.

## Team Startup, continued

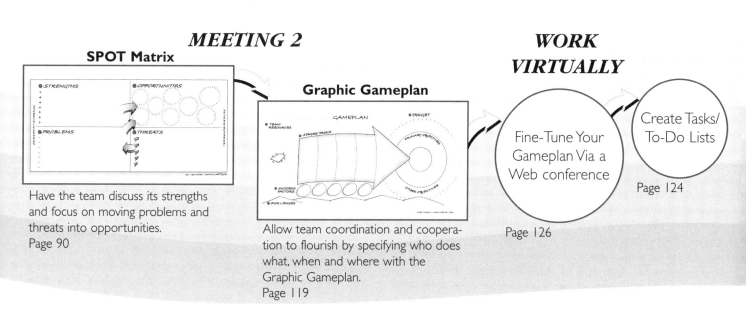

### MEETING 2

**SPOT Matrix**

Have the team discuss its strengths and focus on moving problems and threats into opportunities.
Page 90

**Graphic Gameplan**

Allow team coordination and cooperation to flourish by specifying who does what, when and where with the Graphic Gameplan.
Page 119

### WORK VIRTUALLY

Fine-Tune Your Gameplan Via a Web conference
Page 126

Create Tasks/ To-Do Lists
Page 124

### Page-at-a-Glance Practices

This section of the book is organized with the best practices described in a Page-at-a-Glance format. This format allows you to scan through and quickly find the activity you need. You can photocopy individual pages and literally rearrange the order in which you plan to use them (any other kind of copying must be by permission).

**Useful in a Virtual Meeting**

**Common Name for the best practice**

**Key Benefit**

**General Description used to introduce the practice to a group**

**Tips indicate common variations and challenges**

**Steps involved in leading the practice**

**Stage of *Team Performance* in which practice is most likely to be used**

**Time estimate**

**Illustration shows chart examples and other tools that support the practice, or illustrations of people when the activity is primarily verbal in nature**

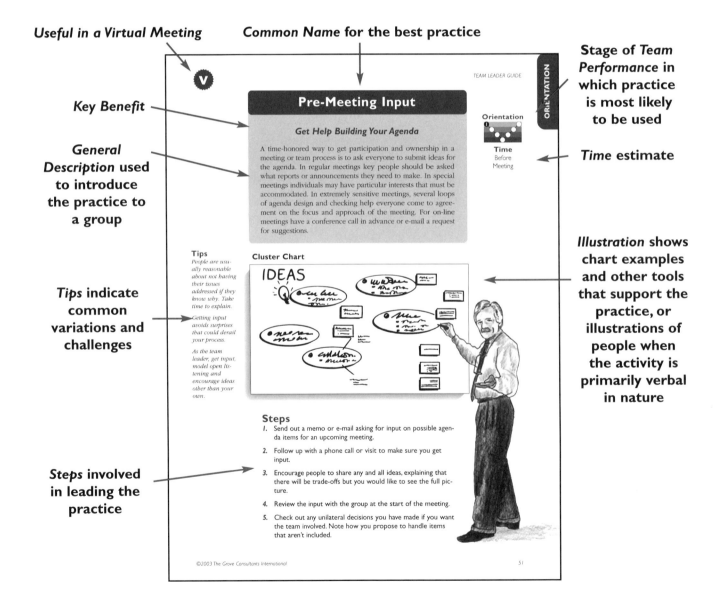

*TEAM LEADER GUIDE*

**ORIENTATION**

## Pre-Meeting Input

### Get Help Building Your Agenda

A time-honored way to get participation and ownership in a meeting or team process is to ask everyone to submit ideas for the agenda. In regular meetings key people should be asked what reports or announcements they need to make. In special meetings individuals may have particular interests that must be accommodated. In extremely sensitive meetings, several loops of agenda design and checking help everyone come to agreement on the focus and approach of the meeting. For on-line meetings have a conference call in advance or e-mail a request for suggestions.

**Orientation**

**Time**
Before Meeting

**Tips**
*People are usually reasonable about not having their issues addressed if they know why. Take time to explain.*

*Getting input avoids surprises that could derail your process.*

*As the team leader, get input, model open listening and encourage ideas other than your own.*

**Cluster Chart**

IDEAS

**Steps**
1. Send out a memo or e-mail asking for input on possible agenda items for an upcoming meeting.

2. Follow up with a phone call or visit to make sure you get input.

3. Encourage people to share any and all ideas, explaining that there will be trade-offs but you would like to see the full picture.

4. Review the input with the group at the start of the meeting.

5. Check out any unilateral decisions you have made if you want the team involved. Note how you propose to handle items that aren't included.

©2003 The Grove Consultants International

51

# Agenda Template

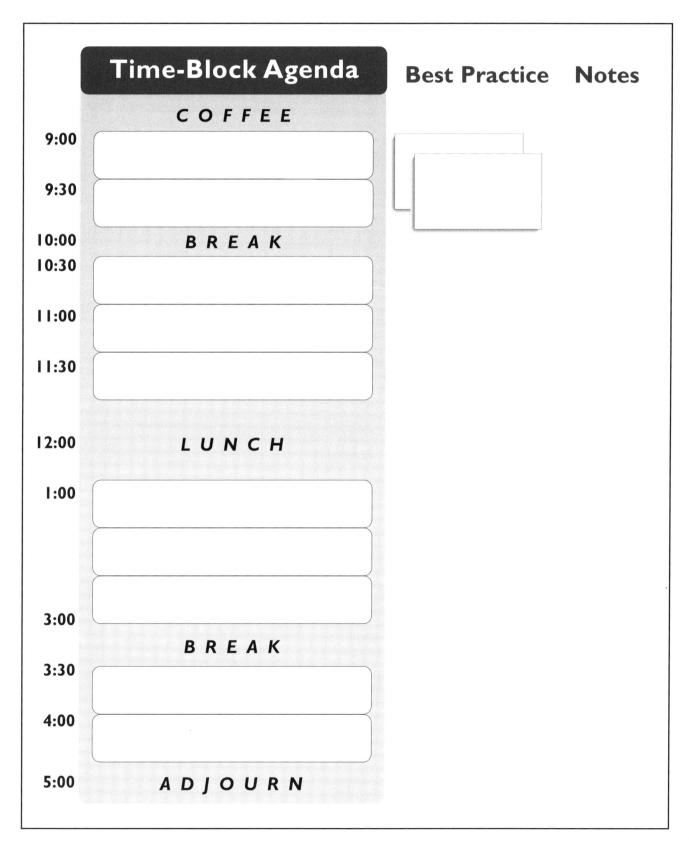

# Practice Template

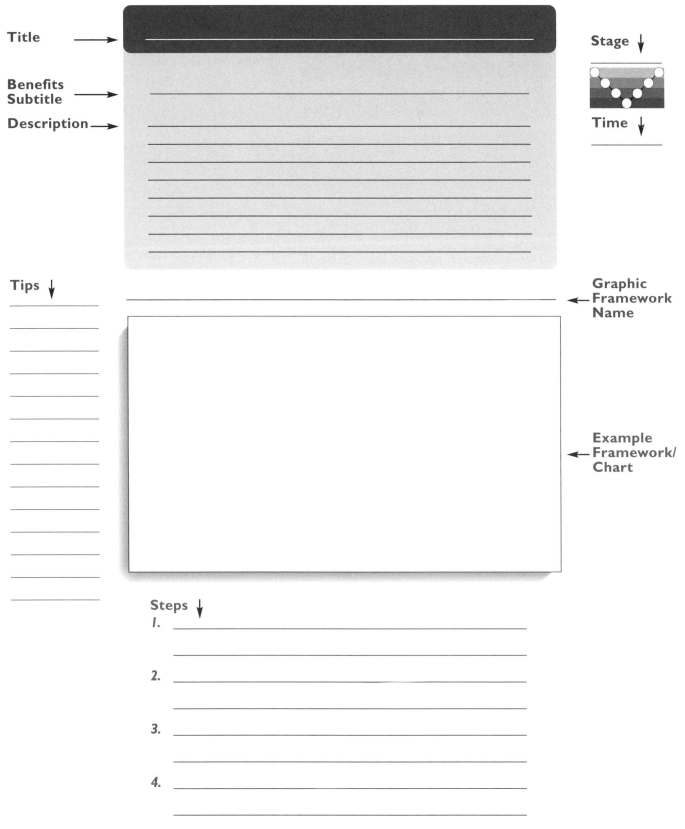

Title →

Benefits
Subtitle →

Description →

Stage ↓

Time ↓

Tips ↓

Graphic
Framework
Name ←

Example
Framework/
Chart ←

Steps ↓
1.

2.

3.

4.

# Graphic Templates

## *Guide Discussions with Prestructured Frames*

Many of the practices in this guide suggest using graphic frameworks to help gather and capture relevant information. Graphic templates are large, visually interesting wall displays that a team fills out as a way to structure its work. They are meant to be used with felt-tip markers during team processes such as brainstorming or problem solving, or online with white boards or Tablet PCs. Graphic templates usually contain an overall metaphor that integrates the elements visually, and categories of items to consider.

**Benefits:**

*Keep the process on track.*

*Encourage participation.*

*Foster creativity by prompting new connections among important elements.*

*Ensure all contributions are acknowledged.*

*Help prioritize elements.*

*Provide a memorable record of what was achieved.*

### Tree of Life Template

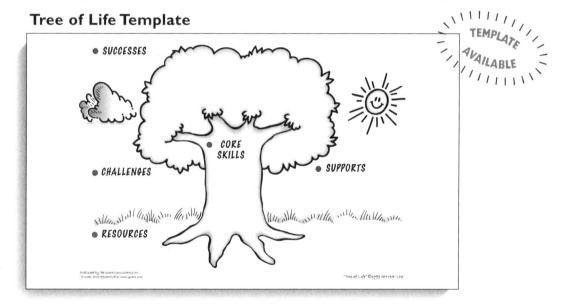

## Steps

1. Determine the desired outcome and pick a graphic framework that will support this outcome.

2. Draw the framework on newsprint or flip-chart paper, or call The Grove to order, purchase pre-printed templates online (www.grove.com), or create your own PowerPoint® templates for on-line work.

3. Hang or load the templates before your meeting.

4. Carefully explain the categories and metaphor to the team.

5. Ask a team member to be the recorder, or volunteer to do the recording yourself.

6. Map the information from the discussion onto the template.

7. If appropriate, use the template to share your work with others.

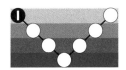

# I. Orientation Stage

## *Why Am I Here?*

Teams all start with some purpose—some person or group is trying to get others involved meaningfully in working together. To begin, you will need to address three areas of concern.

### Getting Started

Team processes are always taking place in the context of other priorities and processes. Sorting out the purpose, outcomes, membership, and levels of investment people will make in any specific team process requires jumping in and getting started. The practices here are the typical things a leader needs to do at the very beginning of any team process or before any meeting.

### Inviting Membership

The research that informed the TPM showed that people are concerned early on about whether or not they fit into a team process and whether or not others will accept them meaningfully. The practices here allow people to address both these concerns.

### Communicating Purposes

The bottom-line goal for orientation is communicating purposes clearly. The practices included here deal with various approaches to communicating a direction and focus for team work, once it has been clarified in the Getting Started activities.

# ORIENTATION PRACTICES

# Pre-Meeting Input

## *Get Help Building Your Agenda*

A time-honored way to get participation and ownership in a meeting or team process is to ask everyone to submit ideas for the agenda. In regular meetings key people should be asked what reports or announcements they need to make. In special meetings individuals may have particular interests that must be accommodated. In extremely sensitive meetings, several loops of agenda design and checking help everyone come to agreement on the focus and approach of the meeting. For online meetings have a conference call in advance or e-mail a request for suggestions.

**Orientation**

**Timing**
Before meeting

## Tips
*People are usually reasonable about not having their issues addressed if they know why. Take time to explain.*

*Getting input avoids surprises that could derail your process.*

*As the team leader, get input, model open listening and encourage ideas other than your own.*

**Cluster Chart**

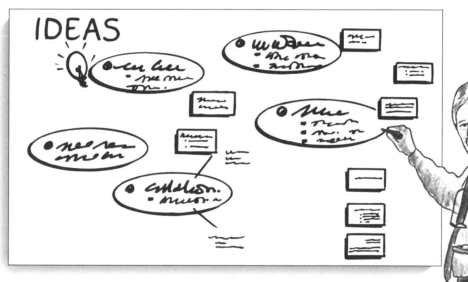

## Steps

1. Send out a memo or e-mail asking for input on possible agenda items for an upcoming meeting.

2. Follow up with a phone call or visit to make sure you get input.

3. Encourage people to share any and all ideas, explaining that there will be trade-offs but you would like to see the full picture.

4. Review the input with the group at the start of the meeting.

5. Check out any unilateral decisions you have made if you want the team involved. Note how you propose to handle items that aren't included.

# Personal Interviews

**Orientation**

**Time**
15–20
minutes each

## Allow People Time to Think Ahead

Personal interviews serve many purposes. A critical one is giving people a private way to express hopes and fears about a process. By asking people what a complete success would look like, you begin seeding a forward-looking energy into the process. By asking people what would waste their time, you get advice on what to avoid and dispel the energy of potential conflict. You also get a chance to share any ideas or information that the group as a whole should know in advance.

**Tips**

*Humor people if they seem resistant. Frame the interview as your wanting to be as helpful as possible.*

*Don't make deals in response to individuals. Team leadership involves serving the whole team.*

*Let people with major complaints have a full hearing. Just listening is powerfully facilitative.*

## Steps

1. Contact team members and arrange for an interview. Say that you would like to get their ideas about the subject at hand and address any questions they have.

2. Keep the questions simple. Share the relevant purpose as you know it, and any other applicable information.

3. Say—"Without regard to being practical, what would be a total success from your point of view if you imagined we were completely finished with the meeting (or process)?"

4. Then say—"Anything we should avoid?"

5. Respond in a way that communicates that you heard what was said.

# Process Design Meetings

## Get Stakeholder Involvement Early

Meetings, offsites, team launches and, especially, longer change processes benefit from being well designed. Involve key people such as your manager, informal leaders, and even skeptics in a pre-meeting to design the process. This will ensure that you begin with a core group that is invested in the process. Good process design meetings minimize misunderstandings and support productivity and creativity.

**Orientation**

**Time**
2–3 hours

**Tips**
*Work graphically on a large time-block agenda display to make the meeting come alive.*

**Time-Block Agenda**

## Steps

1. Identify the outcomes of your process.

2. Describe who should be involved and their interests.

3. Brainstorm what a successfully completed meeting would look like.

4. Identify potential activities and other elements on sticky notes, or type into your online template.

5. Create a blank agenda framework and sketch in times and constraints.

6. Explore possible sequence of elements.

7. Assign roles, including someone to write up the draft agenda.

8. Circulate the agenda in advance of the meeting.

# E-mailed Agendas

**Orientation**

**Time**
1 hour

## Tips

*Make sure you have a name in the subject area of your e-mail program that communicates the purpose of the meeting.*

*If you want to be especially graphic, create the agenda in a layout program and save it as a .pdf file that can be read by Acrobat Reader. This will ensure that it e-mails easily.*

*If you have an organizational network, post the agenda and relevant information on a website and send a brief summary of the meeting and an intranet URL that people can click to get more information.*

## Remind People of Your Meetings

Get in the habit of sending out an agenda in advance of any meetings. People are busy and appreciate having the reminder. If you spend a little extra time producing an agenda that attracts attention and seems inviting, it actually gets the process started before people arrive. For web conferences, it is essential to include times, log-in codes, and a good description of any pre-work required.

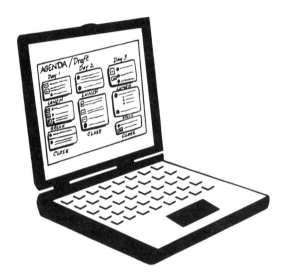

## Steps

1. Write up your agenda, using charts from a design meeting or other notes.

2. Begin with the name of the meeting and the purpose.

3. Indicate the desired outcomes at the top.

4. List different elements you intend to cover in a bullet list or with times.

5. End with a short description of the kind of participation you are looking for from attendees.

# Introductions

## Take Time for People to Engage as People

Group research suggests that people need to trust who they are meeting with to progress with their work. While there are wide variations in different cultures for establishing relationships, it is always important to leave time for people to engage with each other. Following is a checklist of different common introduction activities.

**Orientation**

**Time**
.5–1 hour

### Tips

*Match the time you spend to the length of the process. If people are going to work together for a long period of time, taking time to get to know each other is well worthwhile.*

*In offsites and special workshops, have an evening event around a meal and make introductions the whole point of the gathering.*

*On teleconferences ask everyone to create a graphic seating chart during introductions.*

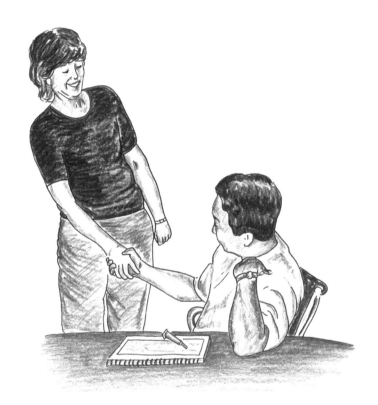

## Options

❏ Share names, jobs and organizations.

❏ Ask everyone to answer a relevant question, such as "What are your hopes and fears?" Or ask everyone to answer a fun question, such as "Share your favorite childhood game."

❏ Have everyone bring a special object that symbolizes something about themselves.

❏ Pick an image from a set of pictures that says something about yourself.

❏ Interview a partner and introduce them.

❏ Share where you grew up.

❏ Share what you hope to get out of this meeting.

❏ Post digital pictures in a web-conference program and refer to them during a go-around.

# Acknowledgements

**Orientation**

**Time**
15 minutes

## Honor Important People and Events

It is common to acknowledge important people who are part of any process. Traditional cultures wouldn't think of meeting without acknowledging elders and those who came before. Public meetings usually acknowledge elected officials and other dignitaries. It helps in any process to give thanks to sponsors, people who worked hard to get everyone together, and those who created special events or developments that made the current event possible. It is also important to acknowledge special circumstances that might be on everyone's mind—say, a natural catastrophe or tragedy of some sort.

**Tips**
*Very formal processes have elaborate protocols for acknowledgement. If you find yourself working in such a setting, seek advice.*

*In some cases special ceremonies are appropriate.*

*In web conferences, it is especially important to reference people by name.*

## Steps

1. Think about who worked to make your meeting or event possible and who is present who needs to be acknowledged.

2. Find out what needs to be said about them if you are going to do introductions.

3. Make a list of people or events needing acknowledgement.

4. Take a few moments at the beginning of any process to recognize these people and events.

# Check-Ins

## Give People Space to Get Present

When people come to a meeting they bring with them a full load of previous experiences, often still circulating around in their feelings and imagination. This is true in meetings at work, and each day during an offsite meeting. To help people get present in your meeting, have everyone "check in" and share what is going on for them. This can be personal or professional information, depending on the trust level of the group. It is sign of respect for the larger lives we lead to simply ask people to reflect on what they would like to share that will help others understand what is going on.

**Orientation**

**Time**
.5–1 hour

## Tips

*Avoid pushing people during a check-in. It should feel invitational, not confrontational.*

*In a multi-day meeting, morning or late afternoon check-ins allow team members to stay connected to what others are actually experiencing.*

*Encourage people to surface any personal issues or concerns that might be standing in the way of doing the work.*

"I have been working with a particularly difficult client..."

"My daughter is graduating from high school tomorrow!"

"I closed a very important deal this morning."

## Steps

1. Suggest that it would be good to take a bit of time to find out what is going on with everyone before starting work.

2. Set a rough time frame.

3. Perhaps start the check-in yourself with a brief overview of what you would like the group to know about.

4. Facilitate the meeting so that everyone has a chance to talk.

5. Record the information if people are raising concerns or items that need attention.

# Expectations

## Orientation

**Time**
20 minutes

### Get Participation from the Beginning

Asking their expectations signals to team members your intent to be facilitative. You can ask about expectations in any number of ways, such as informal phone calls, quick hall conversations, e-mails, formal surveys, or having the meeting start at the beginning by listing expectations. The message should be—"Your ideas are welcome, and this process is here to serve you."

## Tips

*It's useful to let the team know what you intend to do in response to hearing their expectations.*

*Asking about expectations allows you to deal with unrealistic or misinformed expectations before getting too far into a process.*

### EXPECTATIONS

* Finish our quarterly workplan
* Get to know Mark
* Set priorities for next week
* Review the press release

## Steps

1. Think about who is going to be involved in your process.

2. Imagine being in their shoes. Are there any things you might need to check out with them before you begin?

3. Select an appropriate way to make contact, and ask about expectations.

4. Say something like—"Before we begin our process, I'd like to hear about your expectations."

5. Write all of these down, and either begin your meeting with a review of what you have found, or record expectations on a chart right on the spot.

# Desired Outcomes

## Check Direction

Create a chart or slide showing everyone's desired outcomes or objectives. This acknowledges each person's goals in the context of the broader team direction. It helps the team trust its overall direction and allows leaders to check goals with the group. It also gets interests out early and prevents derailments later on in the process.

**Orientation**

**Time**
1 hour

## Tips

*Encourage people to list intangible outcomes as well as measurable objectives.*

*Note that this practice involves sharing desired outcomes. It may take some discussion to decide which are going to be adopted as commitments.*

*The key value of this practice is in getting people to understand each other's interests.*

*Avoid evaluation at this point. Focus on "Is this a real desire?" on the team member's part.*

**Mandala Chart**

## Steps

1. Begin by reviewing the stated goal of the meeting or team process.

2. Write this goal in the middle of a large chart on the wall or on a web-conference white board.

3. Ask team members to think about all the other outcomes they would like, both professional and personal.

4. Write these outcomes clustered around the central goal.

5. Discuss each for understanding.

# OARRs

**Orientation**

**Time**
15–30 minutes

## Begin Meetings with Outcomes, Agenda, Roles and Rules (OARRs)

Setting explicit outcomes focuses meetings and provides a clear direction. Agreement on the agenda gets everyone "in the same boat." Discussing roles and simple rules provides control during the process. Making OARRs explicit increases both trust in the process and participation in getting results. This practice can be done quickly in several sentences or more elaborately with prepared charts or web-conference slides.

**Tips**

*Invite the team to check outcomes and add to them, if need be.*

*To build group discipline, ask the group to agree on an overall agenda before working on specific items.*

*Share ground rules from successful past experience.*

**Meeting Startup Graphic Guide®**

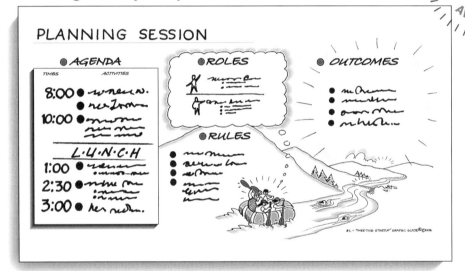

## Steps

1.  List desired outcomes in advance or draw them from the group.

2.  Identify possible activities and sequence them in general time blocks to make a graphic agenda.

3.  Agree on roles.

4.  Review general rules—ask "What will contribute to a successful meeting?"

See the *Meeting Startup Leader's Guide* for detailed instructions on how to use this Graphic Guide (www.grove.com).

# Envisioning Success

## Start Out with the End in Mind

Being able to imagine something happening is the first step toward making it happen. This practice invites everyone to imagine the process completed with results achieved. It anchors people in a positive state of mind at the beginning of a process and allows everyone to share expectations in a collaborative way. It also honors people's intuition, which is the principal faculty that is used to gain foresight in a situation. Using graphics to record people's ideas in a way that can remain posted further deepens the potential of this practice.

**Orientation**

**Time**
1 hour

## Tips

*Conduct this practice at a slower pace than you would normally talk.*

*Talk in the past tense when you are asking about the process.*

*Keep the visioning to positive outcomes. Avoid negatives.*

*Touch on all the senses.*

*When charting the results, note key ideas and images quickly. Support the flow.*

*Remember that some people envision broad vistas while others imagine details.*

*Use chat functions if you are in a web conference and don't feel comfortable with the white board.*

## Mandala Chart

## STEPS

1. Ask everyone to remember a recent process or project that went well.

2. Retain this feeling and focus on a time when the current process will be completed.

3. Ask everyone to visualize the results.

4. Ask everyone to imagine what people are saying.

5. Ask everyone to remember what feels good.

6. Invite people to accept the insights in each idea and share their insights.

7. Record these ideas on a chart.

# Charter Clarification

**Orientation**

**Time**
.5–1 hour

## Agree on the Team's Overarching Purpose

As you begin work, your team needs to agree on its charter so that everyone will be working within the same framework. This helps to accomplish tasks smoothly. This practice asks team members to stay linked to sponsors and the larger enterprise. The team works until everyone is clear about purpose and direction. The charter should be revisited after goal setting and perhaps transformed into a mission to which everyone commits. This is especially important for virtual teams without the reinforcement of regular communications.

**Tips**
*Take as much time as needed to answer questions at this stage or arrange for answers to be obtained.*

*Post the charter in the office for all to see.*

*Publish it for later reference.*

**List Chart**

## STEPS

1. Introduce the process and make it clear that the aim is to clarify the purpose as reflected in the team charter or initiating request.

2. Ask members to write on newsprint or log into an online chat function their perception of what the team charter means.

3. Ask the group to observe common themes.

4. Go around the group and make changes and edits, focusing on details that make the charter clear and vibrant.

5. Keep working until everyone is clear.

# Sharing the Big Picture

## Help Your Team Understand the Larger Context of Its Work

Aligning your team's goals with those of the organization depends on your team having a good grasp of both the market environment in which it is operating, and the organization's vision and strategies that have been established to address the marketplace.

**Orientation**

**Time**
1.5–2 hours

## Tips

*As team leader your role in this process is to facilitate clarification and understanding. Aggressively defending a corporate position that is being challenged will inhibit this process.*

*Do not distance yourself from organizational strategies and make them "their strategies." Your role is to provide the leadership needed to translate higher-level strategies into meaningful action within your scope of responsibility.*

*Accompany web-conference presentations with chat and Q & A to keep people engaged.*

ORGANIZATIONAL GOALS

## STEPS

1. Make sure you are fully conversant with the organization's current vision, strategies and priorities.

2. Set up a meeting to share and discuss this information with your staff. This is particularly useful when doing goal setting with your staff.

3. If appropriate, invite a senior manager to join the meeting to provide a summary and respond to questions.

4. Include in the process an open discussion of key trends and uncertainties in the marketplace for your products or services. Use relevant external sources of trend information to test team assumptions.

5. Facilitate an open discussion of the implications for your team and its work of these big-picture perspectives (see Context Mapping, page 85).

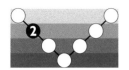

# 2. Trust Building Stage

## *Who Are You?*

Right after getting oriented, team members want to know whom they are working with and what expectations they will have. Although the core issue at this stage is Trust, there are other dimensions as described below.

### Building Mutual Regard

Teams where everyone respects one another work much better than ones where members are cautious, untrusting and disrespectful. It is very helpful to have a good set of best practices for helping members start out with as much regard for each other as possible. This will include learning about each other's backgrounds, interests, and concerns. This is especially critical for virtual teams.

### Increasing Participation

Beyond trust, teams need to have members actively participating, willing to share information and feelings, and being forthright about whatever needs to be communicated. Teams and individuals differ widely in their styles in this regard. This section includes a spectrum of the types of practices leaders can use to get members involved.

### Exploring Competencies

Critical to any team's performance are competent members who can rely on each other. Beyond issues of personal trust, it is important to explore the real content and expertise that everyone brings, and to lay the groundwork for the group to become a real team in the future. Appreciating differences and synergies is the goal of this set of practices.

GO AHEAD AND JUMP! THE GROUP WILL SUPPORT YOU!

# TRUST BUILDING PRACTICES

# Setting Ground Rules

## Agree on Requirements for a Safe Environment

Help people feel safe by drawing out information about what they need to participate fully. In this practice you directly ask what people need in order to trust the group process, and chart these answers on a display that everyone can see. Then ask the group to discuss the ideas until it has a sense of which norms are most important and which are agreed upon by everyone on the team. If online, conduct a go-around to get everyone's ideas.

**Trust Building**

**Time**
2 hours

**TRUST BUILDING**

## Tips
*This practice can be done simply or more in depth, depending on how important it is to have clarity among team members.*

*Taking time for discussion is critical.*

*Revisiting the norms now and then is important if they are to have continuing force for the group.*

TO FEEL SAFE
I NEED...
- Time to respond to questions
- Listening
- Respect for our differences
- No personal attacks
- Time to share feelings

## Steps
*1.* Provide time for members to reflect on what they personally need to trust the team or process. Ask everyone to define needs in behavioral terms.

*2.* Record the answers on a chart or on-line white board, remaining faithful to the key words people used.

*3.* Number the items and discuss for understanding.

*4.* Ask everyone to indicate which are essential for trust.

*5.* Chart and post these norms in the team room or meeting place.

# Identifying Critical Issues

**Trust Building**

**Time**
2–3 hours

## Base Your Work on Real Concerns

Retain an impartial consultant or neutral facilitator to interview all team members about issues that need addressing during a key team startup or planning session. Ask the consultant to feed this information back to the team without attribution, perhaps preceded by a written report. Then have people discuss and perhaps identify their connection with the issues. This kind of survey-data feedback is an effective way of getting around taboos and ignored areas, providing highly valid data with which to catalyze change. It is especially helpful at the start of any strategic visioning or change processes.

## Tips

*Encourage people to own their comments during the feedback session.*

*Give people time to reflect on the information before acting on it.*

*There are a growing number of online surveys that can provide immediate feedback on what everyone is thinking.*

*Polling functions in web conference programs can help rank issues.*

## Steps

1. Retain a consultant with experience in doing surveys.

2. Review the questions you wish to ask with the consultant.

3. Conduct confidential interviews.

4. Hold a meeting with the leader or sponsor to review results.

5. Present to the group involved and discuss the issues raised.

6. Brainstorm possible responses.

7. Organize an action plan.

# Sharing Backgrounds

**Trust Building**

**Time**
1–1.5 hours

TRUST BUILDING

## Build Mutual Respect

If people in your team will be working together for a while, it might be worth having everyone share their backgrounds in a storytelling session. You can focus the practice in many different ways. The intent is to have people share highlights of key experiences that would bear on the work underway. If using web conferences, have everyone create some special slides in advance of the meeting with images and interesting information and use these to support a round of sharing.

## Tips
*Specify the parts of people's backgrounds you want shared. Some people can go on and on.*

*Tell people in advance if you think you may need to cut them off because they are taking more than the allotted time.*

*Don't put anyone on the spot. Let them seek their own level of disclosure at this stage.*

## Steps
1. Point out that it might be helpful to know about each other's backgrounds since "We'll be working together for a while."

2. Initiate the process by sharing yours, featuring the type of information you would like from others.

3. Let each person have a turn sharing his or her background.

4. Create a chart only if you think it is important to see everyone's backgrounds together.

5. Encourage people to ask each other questions.

**Trust Building**

**Time**
2 hours

# History Mapping

## *Show How You Got to Where You Are*

Reviewing the team's history is a natural way of bringing new members into a group. Record the storytelling with text and graphic illustrations on a big timeline to support a rousing exchange that maps the ups and downs of a process. History mapping provides everyone with time to rethink the purpose of the team and the need for new members. It is a very effective practice for cross-functional teams whose members have different perspectives. The graphic storytelling allows room for all points of view and a nonlinear remembering process. Once the stories start, let them be the focus; use the chart as a device to pull out more information.

## Tips

*Leave room at the beginning of the chart for pre-history.*

*Encourage "veterans" to tell how things got started.*

*Include difficult periods.*

*If you have time to prepare, select a graphic metaphor to organize the big picture.*

*A variation on this practice would be to draw part of the history in advance.*

*Let go of any ideas you have about making a neat display. Let the verbal storytelling dominate.*

### Graphic History Graphic Guide®

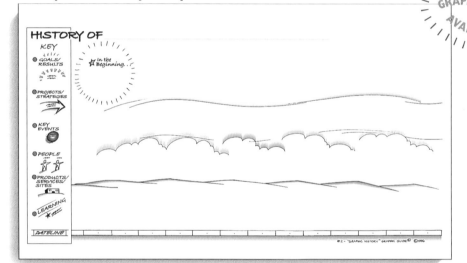

## Steps

1. Make sure people who know the history are present. If possible review with one member beforehand to get mapping ideas.

2. Hang a long sheet of paper. Print out the title of the history and mark out a time line. (Save time by using The Grove's Graphic History Graphic Guide.)

3. Ask someone to remember the beginning of the process, project or organization you are reviewing.

4. Use short questions to draw out the story.

5. Illustrate the story, using various pictographs and graphics.

6. Let the story lead the recording.

7. Encourage people in the group to contribute.

See the *Graphic History Leader's Guide* for detailed instructions on how to use this Graphic Guide (www.grove.com).

# Brainstorming

## Accept Any and All Ideas

Generating new ideas is the purpose of brainstorming. This practice most productively focuses on a single topic with an invitation to all members of the group to share anything that comes to mind, whether or not it seems relevant. Everyone is encouraged to either build on previous ideas or add new ones without evaluating any of the prior comments. All ideas are usually recorded on a chart or online white board for future reference.

## Tips

*Convey interest and excitement during the session.*

*Record what people say the way they say it.*

*Number items only after the list has been completed.*

*Tear pieces of tape or hang paper in advance.*

*If the number of ideas is very large, get someone else to write down every other idea on a separate chart.*

*Write quickly and legibly.*

*Online, use the chat function or white board to brainstorm.*

IMPROVEMENT IDEAS
- Get a schedule board
- Meet more often
- Have shorter meetings
- Keep our agreements
- Write commitments on charts

- Check action items each week
- Conduct an inventory
- Interview each other
- Give awards for performance

## Steps

1. Decide what topic needs brainstorming.

2. Write the focus on a chart or white board.

3. Write the rules for brainstorming on a chart and explain. They are:
   a. Share any idea that comes to mind.
   b. Share only one idea at a time.
   c. Either build on a previous idea or add a new one.
   d. Do not comment on prior ideas.
   e. Do not evaluate ideas during brainstorming.

4. Call on people one at a time.

5. Write all ideas on a chart without evaluation.

**Trust
Building**

**Time**

1 hour

# Personal Bests

## Share Your Standards of Excellence

People deal with new situations confidently when they can link to past successful experiences. This practice builds trust by asking small groups to trade stories about the best experiences they have had related to the work they are beginning. "Bests" are de facto standards for performance, and sharing them lets everyone appreciate the diversity of expertise present in any group. The content focus can be best leadership experiences, team experiences, task group experiences or whatever else is relevant.

### Tips

*Groups of five or six work best.*

*Explain the schedule carefully and set up timekeepers so that everyone has equal time.*

*Coach people to focus on positive feedback about strengths.*

*Link this activity to a full group discussion about the subject at hand.*

*Create a hand-out sheet for notes and feedback.*

*Some web conferences allow breakout sessions. This would be a good practice to use in that way.*

## Steps

1. Allow 15–20 minutes per person, dividing the large group into small breakout groups tailored to how much time you have.

2. Divide into small groups, providing the following process instructions and times:
   a. Begin the session by appointing a timekeeper.
   b. Have one person share a "personal best" for 5–15 minutes.
   c. Have others listen and note personal style of the storyteller and his or her strengths.
   d. Spend five minutes giving feedback. Ask the storyteller to listen without responding.
   e. When everyone is done, list themes.

3. Lead a large group discussion of themes.

# Breakout Groups

## Let Everyone Have a Chance to Talk

People need to participate to feel truly involved in a discussion. This is difficult in large groups, so it is a very effective practice to let pairs, threes, or up to seven people discuss a subject in a small group before inviting large group participation. People usually feel safe in a smaller group. This practice can be used for almost any kind of subject and can be managed in a range of styles, from very loose to focused.

## Tips

*Methods of grouping include turning chairs toward each other, sitting around small tables to begin with, counting off, and pre-assigning clear gathering locations.*

*Invite the group to appoint a facilitator and a reporter.*

*Ask people to introduce themselves to each other.*

*Online breakouts involve having your teleconference operator set up clusters that can talk together. Everyone then logs back on when time is up.*

## Steps

1. Clearly explain the method of grouping you chose (see examples under Tips).

2. Explain the topic of the breakout.

3. Tell people how much time they have.

4. Signal when everyone can start.

5. Let people know when half the time is gone.

6. Alert people when they have just a couple of minutes remaining.

7. Call the breakout to a close and ask people to pay attention up front. Share highlights.

# Report Backs

### Trust Building
### Time
.5–1 hour

## Listen for Shared Themes

Having small groups report back after breakout sessions deepens the connection people have with their conclusions, and allows the group as a whole to experience themes that cut across the groups. Provide clear instructions on the time allowed for the presentations, suggestions for the groups on how to present, and careful moderating. Having groups report-back on graphic templates increases the effectiveness of this practice. It is also possible to have online breakouts show something they've worked on through "application sharing."

## Tips
*Careful structuring of the presentation charts can help reveal patterns you want to look at across a number of groups.*

*Use pairs to discuss themes as a way to get more people involved before a general discussion.*

### TOP FIVE ITEMS

◇ Send manuscript to editor

◇ Incorporate changes by 6/14

◇ Design cover page

◇ Huddle with illustrator

◇ Write press release

## Steps

1. Explain that groups will have a specific amount of time for report-backs after their breakout sessions.

2. Describe any formats you want—like a list of five top items, a filled-out graphic template, a skit, or whatever else you want.

3. Remind small groups to prepare at about 10 minutes before their sessions end.

4. Guide groups to hand in their presentation charts in convenient places.

5. Invite the report-backs.

6. Signal time during presentation.

7. Discuss any themes that the larger group hears.

# Learning Games

**Trust Building**

**Time**
2 hours

**TRUST BUILDING**

## Confront Team Issues in a Fun, Friendly Setting

Games and simulations allow teams to experientially explore group dynamics and other issues that may be too sensitive or complex to address directly. Once the ice is broken with the game, other practices can be used to take action. Games can also be incorporated into meetings, conferences and retreats to generate fun, trust, communication and camaraderie. An easy-to-execute process improvement game is described below.

### Tips

*Allow plenty of time to debrief. People get very animated after an activity.*

*Use fanciful stories as lead-ins to the presentation of a game. Make allusions to work situations.*

*Make sure physical and emotional safety guidelines are covered.*

*You or a team member can take an "observer" role and give neutral feedback to the team.*

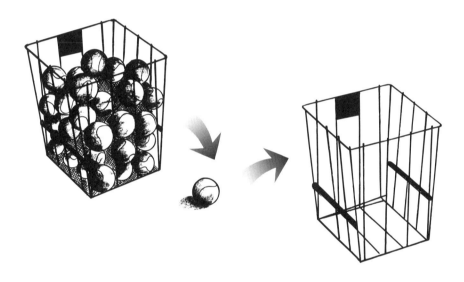

### Steps

1. Identify your desired learning outcomes.

2. Locate a bucket of tennis balls.

3. Divide into two teams of five or more.

4. Explain the goal—"Produce the most tennis balls that you can. To produce a ball it must be touched once by everyone in the team."

5. Ask groups to toss the ball around and set a pattern of touching.

6. Complete a timed run—three minutes.

7. Ask groups to evaluate their process and make improvements.

8. Conduct a second run.

9. Conduct a third run or have everyone discuss learnings. Link to work challenge.

**Trust Building**

**2**

**Time**
2 hours

**Tips**

*Success at dialogue improves by appreciating the mystery of unfolding meaning. Do you believe there is an "implicit order" in our lives that can be discovered through inquiry? Read the quantum physicist David Bohm on this subject.*

*People working with dialogue suggest the following kinds of rules.*
—*Speak your own truth*
—*Suspend judgments*
—*Listen behind what people say for underlying assumptions*
—*Ask questions for inquiry*

# Dialogues

## Look for Underlying Meaning

Discussion is "percussive," often marked by disagreements and quick shifts in conversation. Dialogue seeks to slow down the process and encourage people to listen to each other beyond their specific words to grasp underlying meanings. Participants are encouraged to suspend judgment and ask questions for deeper understanding. An assumption underlying dialogue is that a pattern of group awareness can be unfolded if everyone cooperates in making space for it to emerge. Dialogue is usually focused on an important question that can generate meaningful inquiry. It is most useful when normal discussion doesn't seem to be getting anywhere or when a group is highly interdependent and members need to deeply understand one another.

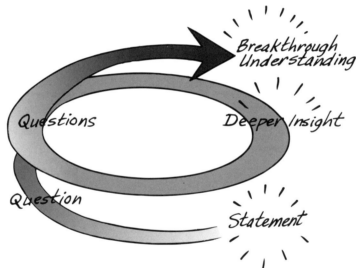

## Steps

1. Suggest using dialogue to draw out deeper understanding in the group.

2. Review the rules for dialogue (see Tips).

3. Ask someone to begin by addressing the central question.

4. Encourage questions that deepen the inquiry.

5. Ask questions yourself that pull out underlying assumptions.

6. Let the dialogue take its own course.

7. Summarize key themes at the end.

# Leader Shares Working Style

## Model Open Exchange

At the start of a challenging process or during a leadership transition in a workgroup, talk directly about your working style and what you would like from the group as a way to build trust. This practice can lead directly into a discussion of how everyone would like others to work with them. It is also a precursor to making commitments in Stage 4 of the Team Performance Model. Dealing with style issues directly, before any problems have occurred, is similar to taking out insurance: team members are less likely to be upset if differences are out in the open from the beginning.

**Trust Building**

**Time**
1 hour

TRUST BUILDING

## Tips

*Encourage team members to share with you what they were used to with the former leader.*

*Use analogies and metaphors that the group understands.*

*If you are uncomfortable with this level of self-disclosure, practice what you will say with a friend.*

## Steps

1. Begin by describing the purpose of this exchange and why you believe it is important for the team.

2. Say clearly what works best for you in regard to communication about problems, suggestions, progress reports, and how decisions are made.

3. Write down the key points for clarity, or prepare slides in advance for online work.

4. Share what clearly does not work and would create confusion or conflict.

5. Invite questions and responses from participants.

# Stakeholder Map

## *Know Whom Your Work Will Impact*

Teams can easily become isolated from their customers—those people who actually have an interest or stake in the work of the team. To help everyone focus on customers or clients, create a stakeholder map. This can be done in many ways. One format involves illustrating rings of involvement depicting the location of those people who are close to the core of a process as well as those who are more on the periphery. The Grove's Stakeholder Map helps to draw out the current and future network of an organization.

**Tips**

*Define the term "stakeholder" as any person or group that has some stake in the outcomes of your team.*

*Write stakeholder names on sticky notes, then move them around until their relationship feels correct.*

*Stretch the group to think of stakeholders who might not be obvious.*

### Stakeholder Map Graphic Guide®

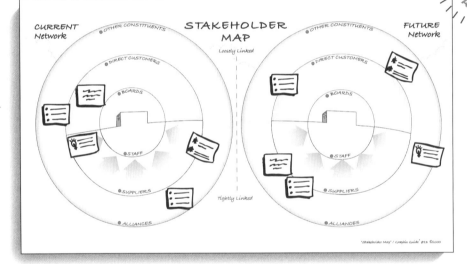

## STEPS

1. Tell a story about the value of being aware of customers and others who have a stake in the work of the team. Brainstorm a list of stakeholders.

2. Hang up a large sheet of paper and put the team name in the center.

3. Draw several rings around the team. Discuss what kind of relationship each ring represents.

4. Mark in the names of people or groups in the rings, discussing the interests they have in the project.

5. Reproduce the stakeholder map for continuing reference and updating.

See the *Stakeholder Map Leader's Guide* for detailed instructions on how to use this Graphic Guide (www.grove.com).

# Team Performance Model

## Make a Case for Spending Time on Trust

The Drexler/Sibbet Team Performance™ Model shows the stages that groups experience as they become teams, and the importance of trust building in the early stages. A framework like this provides a good rationale for spending time on trust building and other fundamental aspects of group process. The model can be introduced quite easily, by explaining that a group needs to gather agreements and understandings around the "why," "who," "what," and "how" questions before it can bounce effectively into implementing and high performance.

## Tips

*A shared framework gives you a shared language. The model doesn't tell you what to do; the people in the group do.*

*Use the metaphor of a "bouncing ball" to get a quick understanding. Groups with a clear purpose need to take on certain constraints and commitments, just like a ball needs a floor or backboard to bounce off to be useful.*

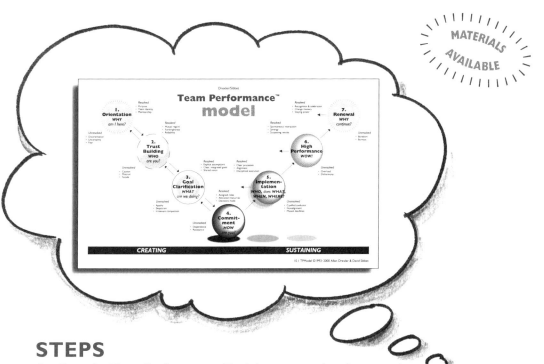

MATERIALS AVAILABLE

## STEPS

1. Post the Team Performance Model poster, or hand out copies.

2. Explain that this model is based on extensive research on the needs groups have in the early stages of team development, and indicates the challenges groups face as they develop.

3. Point out that the graphics and the key words indicate what groups are concerned with at the different stages.

4. Encourage people to explore where they think they are on the model.

5. Explain that issues resolved in earlier stages become the foundation for working things out in later stages. In this sense, trust is fundamental from the second step on.

6. Draw out from the group which stages need attention.

Look to The Grove's materials on Team Performance for more in-depth information about the Team Performance Model.

# 3. Goal Clarification Stage

## *What Are We Doing?*

Being well oriented and trusting the people you are working with clears the way to focus on the specific tasks at hand. At this stage it is natural to want to sort out assumptions, develop a shared vision, and articulate clear goals about the work ahead.

### Drawing Out Information

Any group working together needs a common base of shared information to achieve results. Some of this information is factual, supported by data or experience. Other information is based on assumptions and interpretations that may not be accurate. Identifying all this material is the work of the clarification stage of group process. The practices in this section reflect the special power of graphic visualization to support teams in this work.

### Sharing Vision

As a team works to understand its task, members naturally think ahead and imagine what success would look like. Clarifying the shared vision of a workgroup, team or organization is highly empowering, and helps build the motivation and creative tension to tackle all the challenges and problems that will inevitably arise. Special practices that allow people the chance to articulate their visions are included in this section.

### Clarifying Goals

The TPM research suggests that having clear, integrated goals is one of the strongest predictors of team success. Writing clear goals involves crafting key elements of the group's vision into specific, measurable statements that can be put into action. The practices needed to accomplish this helpful step are explained here.

# GOAL CLARIFICATION PRACTICES

# Voice of the Customer

## *Ensure That Your Team's Goals & Priorities Are Aligned with Those of Your Customers*

If the success of your team ultimately depends on the value you are able to deliver to your customers (external or internal), you need to make sure that you are addressing the needs and interests on which customers place the most importance.

## Tips

*Interviewing a customer can be a defining moment in that relationship, so you want to be sure that team members handle the exchange positively and non-defensively. Consider modeling an interview for your team members and having them practice an interview.*

*For team members who are insulated from your customers, this process can be a powerful tool for getting them directly engaged. Don't let them opt out of the interview process unless there is an over-riding reason.*

WE WOULD LIKE TO FIND OUT HOW WE CAN SERVE YOU BEST.

## Steps

1. Meet with your team to propose this process for gathering customer feedback. As a team, discuss which customers you need to interview and what you need to learn from them.

2. Jointly develop a set of questions to ask your customers regarding their problems, needs, interests and level of satisfaction with your product/service.

3. Organize team members to interview specific customers using these questions.

4. Jointly analyze the customer responses, summarizing them with short statements written on sticky notes for sorting.

5. Cluster the statements into categories and prioritize the categories by urgency and importance.

6. Develop a set of goals to address the priority items.

## Goal Clarification

**Time**
2 hours

## Tips

*Focus audio-graphic conferences on gathering input from everyone, not decision making. Have a smaller team take the input and propose a decision, and hold a second conference to check it out.*

*Most electronic white board tools are clumsy for active recording of a lot of words. Tablet PCs supported by a drawing program yield the best results.*

*Common choices of tools include:*
*—Web conferencing software using direct white-board or visualizer inputs.*
*—Teleconferencing using a common website.*

*Develop a contingency plan beforehand in the event of technical difficulties.*

# Web Conferences

## See the Work—Hear Your Colleagues

Web conferencing is a teleconference married to a graphic computer display. Sometimes called audio-graphic conferencing, it is a very productive option for any group or team that is past the trust building stages and wants to focus mainly on the work. There are many kinds of tools available. Most support sharing an electronic white board or computer-generated media. It is also possible to simply talk to people on the telephone while jointly looking at a web site that has graphics. More advanced applications include using graphic visualizers that allow detailed graphic recording in a web conference.

## Steps

1. Determine the kind of tools you plan to use.

2. Call in advance to make sure participants have all the dial-in numbers and passwords.

3. Make sure all participants have downloaded any plug-ins or client software required.

4. Begin the conference with a check-in go-around.

5. Explain the focus of the meeting with a visual or a slide, and describe the way you plan to capture comments.

6. Conduct the conference.

7. Check in with people who have been quiet for a while.

8. Summarize what you have accomplished by reviewing the visuals.

# Context Mapping

## Keep the BIG PICTURE in Mind

All teams work in a context. This means that there are always other things going on: larger environmental forces, history, stakeholders, related projects and organizations. These context factors shape what is and is not possible just as much as the internal capacities and capabilities of a team. Context mapping involves creating a large display of all these factors, usually focusing on the most relevant.

**Goal Clarification**

**Time**
1 hour

**GOAL CLARIFICATION**

## Tips

*Using a landscape metaphor to organize the display will seem intuitively clear to people.*

*Make the category names, trends and factors the same color and bold, with bullets, underlining or highlighting to help them stand out.*

*Ask the group for help in placing information. Have fun with it.*

### Context Map Graphic Guide®

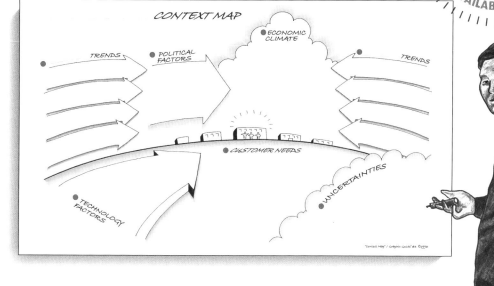

## Steps

1. Hang a Context Map Graphic Guide or a 4-by-8-foot length of poster paper on the wall, or preload in a web-conference program.

2. Ask participants to list individually or in small groups the categories of environmental elements they think are relevant.

3. Select the categories the group wants to review given the time available and the ideas' importance.

4. Use the items as labels for fields of information as illustrated.

5. Facilitate a discussion of key trends and changes under each of these items, and record all information under the heading you have selected.

See the *Context Map Leader's Guide* for detailed instructions on how to use this Graphic Guide (www.grove.com).

6. Make sure you copy the display.

**Goal Clarification**

**Timing**
During meetings

# Graphic Case Studies

## Visualizing Success Patterns of Other Processes

Take a recent team experience or project and diagram its history to see how people succeeded in situations similar to yours. These sessions can achieve several objectives. You can identify potential roles, anticipate challenges, identify activity cycles, and the like. The graphic approach facilitates seeing things in context and appreciating the interdependency of different stages in group process.

## Tips

*Imagine the chart as a series of flows representing the attention, energy, information and operations of the process.*

*Remember that the display is simply a support for the storytelling. The central value of this practice is to give people a chance to tell stories about their roles and responsibilities, for greater understanding.*

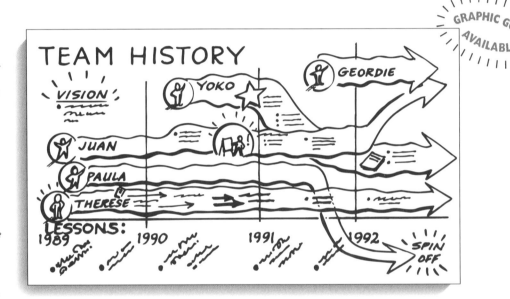

## Steps

1. Create a time line on the wall.

2. Ask the person with the longest experience to tell the story of how the team got started. Ask for a description of his or her role.

3. Ask each person to identify when he or she joined the team and in what role. Encourage them to describe their experience on the team.

4. Keep a list of any action issues on a flip chart.

5. Along the bottom of the chart, note lessons learned.

6. Reproduce the chart to provide a memory boost.

Use a Graphic History Graphic Guide® from The Grove Consultants International (www.grove.com) if you want a template for this practice.

# Analog Brainstorming

## Compare with Similar Situations to Suggest Solutions to Yours

Many creative insights arise from seeing parallels between the specific challenge you face and a challenge in a completely different domain that had similar characteristics, such as sports, performance arts, or other types of organizations. By exploring solutions in a parallel situation, breakthrough ideas can be uncovered that apply to the challenges you face.

**Goal Clarification**

**Time**
2 hours

## Tips

*If your challenge is complex, it is helpful to introduce this practice with a simpler example so participants can grasp the value of looking for creative solutions in parallel situations.*

*If the group gets stuck for solutions in one parallel situation, try another.*

*This process is based on a more comprehensive process called Synectics described in the classic* The Practice of Creativity: A Manual for Dynamic Group Problem-Solving, *by George M. Prince.*

## Steps

1. State the challenge in terms that point to its resolution (e.g. "to produce a product version that is invulnerable to incidental damage" instead of "profits are being eroded by excessive returns due to damage").

2. Generate a list of parallel situations with characteristics similar to the stated challenge. Look for situations that are different from the one you are facing.

3. Pick a parallel situation that seems interesting and look for examples of good solutions in that environment. Don't limit yourself to known solutions: brainstorm your own. Encourage participants to be playful and a bit outrageous at this point. Accept all ideas without criticism.

4. Examine the identified solutions. Ask how they can suggest equivalent solutions to your challenge. List all suggestions.

5. Ask participants to identify solutions that have significant potential. Be careful not to dismiss any with the kernel of a breakthrough idea at this point just because they have some drawbacks. Select those with the strongest potential and work on ways to overcome associated drawbacks.

**Goal
Clarification**

**Time**
2 hours

# Slot Machine Brainstorming

## *Play with Combinations of Features to Generate New Options*

When developing a solution to problems, it is easy to get focused on a limited set of options and overlook other options that are readily available. By systematically exploring different ways to combine the options for addressing critical elements of your problem, you can come up with solutions you hadn't considered, and perhaps find one that will be a real breakthrough.

**Tips**

*The process of combining elements in unusual ways helps teams break out of established patterns of thinking.*

*The real creativity comes in finding the hidden value in these unusual combinations.*

*This process works best if it is done in a purposeful but playful manner. Hold off on evaluation until Step 5. Even then it is helpful to identify at least one thing you like about a new idea before stating your concern.*

## SLOT MACHINE BRAINSTORMING

| Element A | Element B | Element C | Element D |
|-----------|-----------|-----------|-----------|
| Option A1 | Option B1 | Option C1 | (Option D1) |
| Option A2 | Option B2 | (Option C2) | Option D2 |
| (Option A3) | Option B3 | Option C3 | Option D3 |
| Option A4 | (Option B4) | Option C4 | Option D4 |

## Steps

1.  Identify all the elements that are critical to a viable solution of your problem. Consider not only the physical elements such as tools and materials but also elements arising from the process of doing your work, such as design, fabrication, distribution, use, and disposal.

2.  Create a spreadsheet where each identified element is the heading for a separate column.

3.  In the column for each element, list all the optional ways of handling that element.

4.  Divide participants into pairs or small groups and have each choose one interesting option from each column and combine the options to create a potential solution. Tell them to come up with a plausible story for why their new solution is worth considering.

5.  Report on these new combinations and encourage everyone to listen for potential breakthrough insights.

6.  Have participants identify the compelling ideas that emerged from the previous step and use them to formulate some new viable solutions.

# Force-Field Analysis

## Identify Forces Supporting and Resisting Change

Kurt Lewin, a pioneer in the field of social science, proposed this practice as a way for groups to form a strategy for supporting change. Any new development or proposal has forces that support its happening and forces opposing it. These can be illustrated on a "T" bar, listing SUPPORTING on one side and RESISTING on the other. After listing everything people can think of, rank items as to importance, and take special note of the big resisting forces. Lewin's thesis is that weakening a resisting force is the most effective way to make progress.

**Goal Clarification**

**Time**
1 hour

**GOAL CLARIFICATION**

### Tips
*Doing these charts on a large scale helps everyone see the complete picture.*

*Use graphic arrows pointing into the "T" from each direction in addition to the writing.*

*Use Multi-Voting (page 112) or Dot Voting (page 111) to rank items if the important resisting forces aren't clear.*

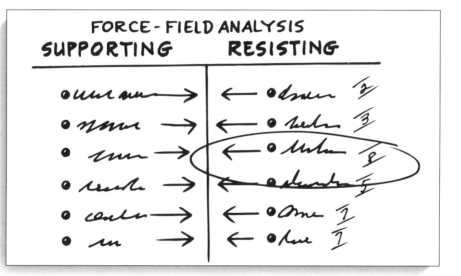

## Steps

1. Hang a long sheet of paper on the wall, or create a template on a web-conference white board, showing a large "T" frame as shown above.

2. Write the focus for the analysis on the top of the chart.

3. Explain Lewin's theory as described above.

4. List all forces supporting the change being considered, and list all forces resisting the change.

5. Rank the forces resisting.

6. Discuss for understanding and pick the most important resisting forces.

7. Brainstorm strategies for weakening the resistance.

**Goal
Clarification**

**Time**
2 hours

# SPOT Analysis

## Identify Strengths, Problems, Opportunities and Threats

Identifying current STRENGTHS and PROBLEMS and future OPPORTUNITIES and THREATS is a good way to generate data about your team's situation and provide a medium in which everyone can compare assumptions. These four perspectives are interrelated, because the best opportunities are those that build on strengths, and the most important problems are small threats. This practice helps your team clarify differences of opinion and discuss problems in context.

## Tips

*Use "+" for STRENGTHS, "-" for PROBLEMS, "*" for OPPORTUNITIES, and lightning or storm clouds for THREATS.*

*A variation has individuals working on their own SPOTs and then sharing.*

*Rank the factors if you have time.*

*Bring out old SPOTs to give the team a sense of progress and change.*

### SPOT Matrix Graphic Guide®

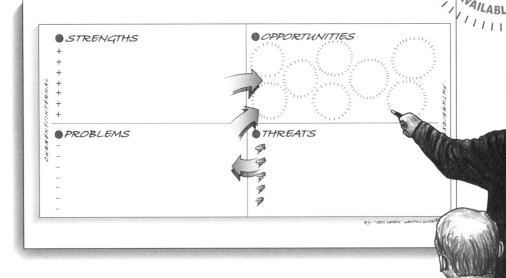

GRAPHIC GUIDE® AVAILABLE

## Steps

1. Hang the SPOT Matrix Graphic Guide on the wall.

2. Clarify desired outcomes for the session.

3. First map the strengths, then the problems.

4. Rank-order the strengths and problems if you have time.

5. Brainstorm opportunities, encouraging people to see problems as potential opportunities for improvement.

6. Discuss and list threats—those factors that could terminate the team or invalidate its work.

7. Review the whole chart for insights.

See the *SPOT Matrix Leader's Guide* for detailed instructions on how to use this Graphic Guide (www.grove.com).

# Cause Analysis

## Use Data to Identify the Cause of Disruptive Problems

Changes in your team's tools, materials, resources, environment or other critical variables can disrupt your successful operation. Identifying the cause of the problem is an essential step in solving the problem. An incorrect diagnosis of the cause can lead to substantial wasted effort trying to fix the problem. Cause analysis involves identifying critical distinctions associated with the problem's occurrence.

**Goal Clarification**

**Time**
3 hours

## Tips

*This process does not work in startup situations where you do not have a track record of satisfactory performance against which to search for distinctions.*

*This process is most successful when applied to situations where the cause can be tracked to some operating variable other than the people involved. Changes in human behavior are less predictable and harder to pin down in this manner.*

*This process is based on a more comprehensive process called* Problem Analysis, *described in the classic,* The New Rational Manager, *by Charles Kepner.*

---

### CAUSE ANALYSIS

| Problem Occurred | No Problem Occurred | Distinctions |
|---|---|---|
| 1. | | |
| 2. | | |
| 3. | | |
| 4. | | |
| 5. | | |
| 6. | | |

---

## Steps

1.  Identify the timing associated with the occurrence of the problem (when it first occurred, when it stopped, when it recurred, etc.)

2.  Identify instances where the problem has not occurred but might have.

3.  Look for distinctions between cases identified in Steps 1 and 2 (where the problem has occurred and where it has not occurred).

4.  Focus on the distinctions identified and ask whether any of these individually or in combination could have logically caused the problem.

5.  Test your conclusion, if practicable, by changing the variables identified and observing the results.

**GOAL CLARIFICATION**

**Goal
Clarification**

**Timing**
Several days

**Tips**
*Field research is an excellent action-learning activity for people in a leadership development track in their organization.*

*Using large graphic templates for reporting invites more discussion than electronic presentations.*

*Creating an original mural challenges the group to really understand its findings.*

*This practice is especially important for managers who have become out of touch with their people.*

# Field Research Teams

## *Build Your Team Through First-Hand Research*

In extremely dynamic situations, where internal and external changes have occurred or need to occur, it becomes very important to do field research. Assigning teams of people to investigate specific topics gives them a chance to learn what is really going on first-hand, challenge assumptions, and form closer relationships with each other. When the teams bring their research findings back, they have a real connection with the information, and will be able to involve their colleagues more deeply. People need valid information about the need to change before they buy into any change process.

## STEPS

1. Identify areas needing research as part of a planning process.

2. Organize teams of people who will benefit from getting to know each other and from doing the research.

3. Provide the teams with a clear charter, including goals, timeline, and a presentation template. Ask them to develop interview questions, questionnaires or observation goals.

4. Contact teams as the time to get engaged nears.

5. Organize a clear time for the teams to report back.

6. Ask the teams to summarize their findings in some kind of graphic display, electronic presentation, or handout.

7. Manage the team reports and the facilitation of question-and-answer sessions.

# Affinity Diagrams

**Goal Clarification**

**Time**
1–2 hours

## Use Sticky Notes to Find Themes

If you want everyone to participate in generating and organizing a lot of information, use sticky notes to create affinity diagrams. There are many variations, but they all involve generating information with one idea or item per card. The cards or sticky notes are then grouped by their "affinities." This process engages the group in thinking through the big themes. The process can be pushed further by asking which of the themes are overarching the others, creating a branching diagram of clustered information.

## Tips

*A fast way to organize the clusters is to let the entire group approach the display and rearrange things. It's messy but engaging.*

*Be prepared to photograph or hand copy the display for reference. A lot of information gets generated.*

*Cards can be marked with headings and collected to be compiled later.*

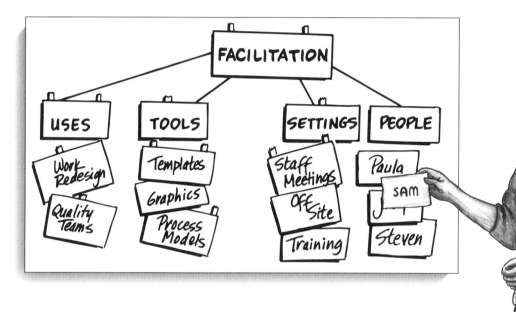

## STEPS

*1.* Agree on the focus of the session with the group.

*2.* Hand out sticky notes or cards.

*3.* Coach people to print clearly (upper- and lowercase preferably), use 2–5 words, and one idea or item per card.

*4.* Post all cards, either one at a time or in clumps. Go over the cards for clarity.

*5.* Cluster the sticky notes into affinity groups. Allow discussion of appropriate headings.

*6.* Identify overarching themes, using polling, dot voting, or some other convergence practice.

*7.* Reorganize the diagram with the big themes on top, and those that branch underneath. Name and circle the clusters.

**Goal Clarification**

**Time**

2 hours

# Vision Exchange

## Share Your Personal Visions

After you have allowed yourself to envision a desired future state, share it with a partner. Then ask the partner to tell you which parts were the most compelling—which seemed convincing and moving. Then listen to his or her vision and give feedback. Find another partner and repeat the process. A third round adds depth and conviction in response to the feedback and further imagining. This sharing also lets your team experience common themes.

## Tips

*Stay focused on the most compelling aspects of the vision. Avoid evaluations.*

*Check to make sure people are talking in the past tense and imagining the vision accomplished.*

*Encourage people to "just make it up" if they seem to have trouble imagining.*

MATERIALS AVAILABLE

## Steps

1. Imagine a compelling future state, using guided imagery.

2. With a partner, take five minutes to share your vision (in the (past tense) as if it were already accomplished. The partner listens for the parts that are most compelling and encourages more detail.

3. Allow three minutes for the listener to say which parts were most compelling to him or her.

4. Reverse the process, encouraging use of the past tense.

5. Take new partners and repeat the full cycle. Get everyone to share some observations between rounds.

6. Repeat a third time for depth.

7. Lead a general discussion on themes.

*See The Compass: A Visual Workbook for Exploring Your Future, The Grove's process for exploring your personal vision. (www.grove.com).*

# Mandala Vision

Goal
Clarification

Time
I hour

GOAL
CLARIFICATION

## Array Vision Elements on a Circular Display

Mandala is an ancient Sanskrit word for archetype, or universal pattern. It usually refers to a circular image that suggests wholeness. A mandala vision is a circular drawing of different aspects or elements of a vision that together represent a picture of a desired future state. Using this format will remind people of the aspirational nature of a vision. Its simple structure is easy to work with and adapt to many different degrees of complexity.

## Tips

*Frame this activity as a first-draft vision, simply gathering agreements so that everyone can think more about it. This frees people to be more imaginative.*

*The Mandala template is a good place to gather shared vision ideas.*

*This framework can also be used for goals and themes or any kind of information clustering where you want to show elements surrounding a central idea.*

## Mandala Vision Graphic Guide®

GRAPHIC GUIDE®
AVAILABLE

## Steps

1. Have pairs or individuals brainstorm vision elements on sticky notes, following whatever exercises you may have conducted to get people into a future frame of mind. (See Vision Exchange, page 94.)

2. Ask for an initial idea and put it on the chart outside one of the circles. Then ask if there are related ideas and cluster them in rays leading out from the circles.

3. When all ideas have been gathered, take one cluster and invite the group to create a statement that sums up the ideas in a compelling way. Use a flip chart as a scratch pad.

4. Once everyone agrees with the statement, write it in a circle.

5. Complete the process around the mandala.

6. See if there is a central integrating statement for the middle.

See the *Mandala Vision Leader's Guide* for detailed instructions on how to use this Graphic Guide (www.grove.com).

## Tips

*As team leader your role in this process is both to carry the banner for the organization's goals as they relate to your team and to engage your team in shaping and refining these goals.*

*Avoid placing yourself in the position of immediately defending the organization's goals against direct or implied criticism. The quality of this process is enhanced by open debate and challenge.*

*Be clear going into this process about what is non-negotiable and what is open to change. This will help your team members know where to direct their attention and energy.*

# Goal Alignment—Top/Down

## Ensure That Your Team's Goals & Priorities Are Aligned with Those of the Organization

An organization's goals and strategies provide vital direction and focus, but they can only be realized when they are translated into specific actions throughout the organization. This practice addresses the process of translating your organization's goals and strategies into relevant goals and priorities for your team.

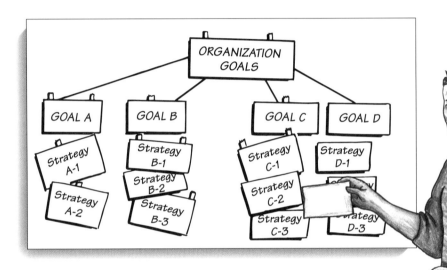

## Steps

1. Review the organization's goals and strategies with your team. (See Sharing the Big Picture, page 63.)

2. Present the goals and priorities you have developed for the team and describe how they align with the organization's goals.

3. Invite members of the team to share their responses, including:

   —elements they support;
   —elements they would like to see modified, added or dropped;
   —challenges and opportunities raised by these goals;
   —how these team goals connect with their own goals.

4. Facilitate a process for refining the original goals based on the team input.

5. Check for consensus. Are these goals that everyone can actively support?

6. Agree on next steps, including the need for horizontal goal alignment. (See Goal Alignment—Horizontal, page 98.)

# Goal Alignment—Bottom/Up

**Time**
1.5–2 hours

## Tips

*As team leader your role in this process is both to carry the banner for the organization's goals as they relate to your team and to engage your team in shaping and refining these goals.*

*Avoid placing yourself in the position of immediately defending the organization's goals against direct or implied criticism. The quality of this process is enhanced by open debate and challenge.*

*Be clear going into this process about what is non-negotiable from the organization's perspective and what is open to change. This will help your team members know where to direct their attention and energy.*

### *Ensure That Your Team's Goals & Priorities Are Aligned with Those of the Organization*

An organization's goals and strategies provide vital direction and focus, but they can only be realized when they are translated into specific actions throughout the organization. This practice addresses the process of aligning your team's goals and priorities with those of the organization at large.

## Steps

1. Review the organization's goals and strategies with your team. (See Sharing the Big Picture, page 63.)

2. Invite members of the team to share their responses, including:

   —current team priorities that support the organization's goals and strategies;

   —challenges and opportunities raised by the organization' goals and strategies;

   —ways the team could redirect its priorities to more strongly support the organization's goals and strategies;

   —how these team goals connect with their own goals.

3. Facilitate a process for identifying and prioritizing team goals based on the organization's goals and strategies. (See related best practices for this step.)

4. Check for consensus. Are these goals that everyone can actively support?

5. Agree on next steps, including the need for horizontal goal alignment. (See Goal Alignment—Horizontal, page 98.)

**Goal
Clarification**

**3**

**Time**
1.5–2 hours

# Goal Alignment—Horizontal

## *Ensure That Your Team's Goals and Priorities Are Aligned with Others Who Impact and Are Impacted by Your Work*

If goal alignment is only done vertically, opportunities for synergies with others whom your team depends on through horizontal relationships can be missed, and differences can go unresolved.

## Tips
*Agree in advance on the process that will be used for goal alignment.*

*If the issues are likely to be complex or the priorities in conflict, it can be helpful to have a neutral facilitator lead the process.*

*Alignment often occurs simply by sharing priorities and flagging opportunities for mutual support.*

## Steps

1. Invite representatives from relevant stakeholder groups to meet with your team to align respective goals and priorities.

2. Review your team's goals with the others.

3. Invite the others to share their relevant goals. Consider capturing each goal on a large sticky note, so that they can be clustered and compared.

4. Identify potential synergies, gaps, overlaps and conflicts. Use the sticky notes to help organize the goals into relevant categories, or type into your online program.

5. Identify ways to achieve alignment.

6. Develop revised goals and test for mutual agreement.

# SMART Objectives

## Be Explicit About Goals

One of the most productive things a group can do is to make its objectives clear. The most direct way involves writing them down on chart paper and posting them clearly. If goals are not clear, guide the group in creating some. Use the SMART acronym for criteria, making the objective statements Specific, Measurable, Action-Oriented, Realistic and Time-Constrained. Everyone should be able to tell when objectives are met.

**Goal Clarification**

**Time**
2 hours

**GOAL CLARIFICATION**

## Tips

*An alternative is to write possible objectives on cards (one per card), then have pairs create a common list. Finally, have the pairs meet as fours and consolidate.*

*Keep objective statements crisp.*

*Objectives can complement and strengthen a vision that may include more elements than members can be truly objective about.*

PRIORITY OBJECTIVES

1. Initiate one new multi-year project for 2+ team members by 9.1

2. Install and field test marketing support system by 12.1

3. Create pers development for all team me by 2.1

4. Initiate monthly team meetings and written reports immediately

## Steps

1. Explain the SMART framework by writing it out on a chart or slide (see description above).

2. Ask everyone to check the team's objective statements against the SMART criteria.

3. Rename the statements to make sure they meet the SMART criteria.

4. Post the revised objectives on chart paper.

5. Reproduce them so that the team can reference them easily from workstations and offices.

**Time**
3+ hours

# Vision and Bold Steps

## Align for Creative Action

Having agreement on an overarching vision of where you are headed and the four or five bold steps you will begin to take immediately provides a clear, high-level framework for action. A bold-steps template avoids the detail of an implementation plan, and offers a good springboard for action planning and road mapping sessions. A strong vision linked to immediate steps creates organizational tension that drives creative action.

## Tips

*This template has a fully developed Grove Leader's Guide if you need more help.*

*Use the areas on the sides of the arrow to keep notes about what supports and challenges forward movement.*

*If your group has time to talk about shared values, record these along the bottom. They are the metaphorical road that supports action.*

*Be prepared to review and update this template a couple of times to get full commitment of a management team.*

**Five Bold Steps Vision Graphic Guide®**

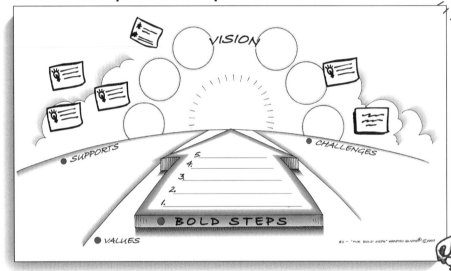

## Steps

*1.* Review the vision brainstorms you have completed.

*2.* Ask pairs to identify candidate shared-vision elements, writing one per sticky note, or entering in an online chart.

*3.* Arrange vision elements in rays around the circles on the top half of the template.

*4.* Determine agreed-on parts of the vision and write them in the circles.

*5.* Define what constitutes a "bold step."

*6.* Ask pairs to identify candidates for bold steps on sticky notes.

*7.* Cluster and agree on key steps.

*8.* Write them in the big arrow.

See the *Five Bold Steps Vision Leader's Guide* for detailed instructions on how to use this Graphic Guide (www.grove.com).

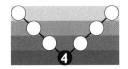

# 4. Commitment Stage

## *How Will We Work Together?*

As goals and shared information become clear, a team will move to the bottom-line considerations of level of commitment, allocation of scarce resources, and determination of key roles. This section includes practices aligned with the most common ways of handling these issues.

### Consensus Decision Making

Facilitative leadership has grown out of groups that work in a consensus fashion. These practices represent ways to get convergence in thinking and decisions that are shared by all members. Consensus is achieved when everyone is able to "live with" and accept a decision as a working agreement.

### Polling

These practices include polling techniques and reviews of the most common forms of traditional voting. In consensus-oriented groups voting is a helpful tool to test the level of agreement and promote dialogue. Polling helps involve people in webconferences.

### Executive Decision Making

Many workgroups and teams have managers in charge with the authority and desire to make key decisions. Executive decisions enable the process when time is precious and organizational support is critical. Different approaches to this are included here.

### Negotiating Roles

People have a stake in what they end up doing on a team or in a group process, even if assigned by managers or selected by a group. There are a spectrum of useful approaches for negotiating agreement about roles.

### Allocating Resources

When agreements are made and roles determined, resources are needed in order to implement. These include time, money, and staff resources, in most cases. Practices for sorting out responsibilities, time commitments and other allocation issues are included here.

# COMMITMENT
# PRACTICES

# Agreeing on Decision Making

## Be Explicit About How Agreements Are Made

To accomplish tasks with any efficiency and productivity, a team must agree on how it makes decisions. One of the most facilitative things you can do as a team leader is to help people be clear about this subject. You may have to provide an overview of options, explaining the differences between consultative, consensus, voting, and executive decision making. Because decisions directly affect the ongoing effectiveness of a team, it is helpful to agree on how they are made.

**Commitment**

**Time**
2 hours

## Tips

*Be clear about which process you are using to make this commitment.*

*Brief new members about the type of decision process you are using.*

*In regular department meetings, consultative and executive decision making is more appropriate, maintaining the authority of the line. In special processes, consensus is widely used. In formal bodies, voting is common.*

CONSENSUS
- Everyone can "work with" the decision.
- Discussion of all issues.

CONSULTATIVE
- Key decision maker accepts input and advice, then acts.

EXECUTIVE
- Decisions designated to single person or team.

VOTING
- Majority or 2/3 "yes" can make decision.

## Steps

1. Create flip charts like those shown above that review the types of decision-making processes, or create a slide for on-line presentation.

2. Lead the group in a discussion of which process best fits the task at hand.

3. Record pros and cons for each one if it is not obvious which will work better, or ask for responses in a chat function.

4. Look at each type and indicate which tasks it would be best for.

5. Hear out individual ideas until the group is clear.

6. Agree on a process for your group.

COMMITMENT

# Checking Against Outcomes

Commitment

**Time**
30 minutes

## Use Outcomes Like a Compass

Meetings and team processes, like real voyages, can get lost if you don't return frequently and check the desired outcomes toward which everyone is working. Managers and team leaders often assume that outcomes are clearer than they are to others. Make sure the outcomes are aligned with formal leadership and the group as a whole. The simplest way to keep direction is to explicitly revisit stated outcomes.

## Tips

*If outcomes were originally general, then be more specific at this point in a process.*

*Ask people which outcomes are getting real attention outside the meetings.*

*Be willing to challenge the outcomes yourself. If they are real, the group will defend them.*

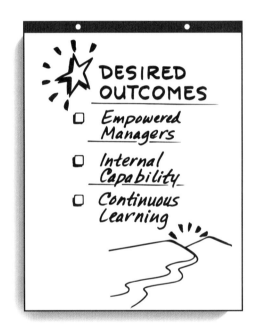

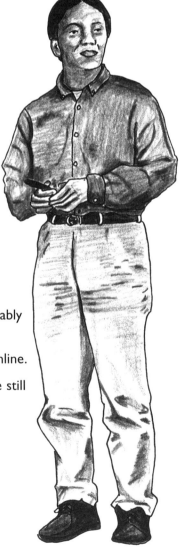

## Steps

1. Find the Outcomes chart or memo that you probably created at the start of your process.

2. Post the outcomes or pull up an outcome slide online.

3. Go through each one and check whether they are still the outcomes everyone wants.

4. Add any new outcomes.

5. Eliminate ones that no longer apply.

6. Rate and rank the outcomes if you a need to set priorities.

# Criteria Grid

**Commitment**

**Time**
1 hour

## Compare Choices with Success Criteria

An analytical way to make decisions is to create a grid comparing options against criteria and search for the best fit. Criteria would include any description of what is needed for success. In manufacturing there are internal quality criteria as well as external customer criteria. Criteria can also be a way of expressing objectives, by reflecting what you want as a result of a decision or an activity. The process of constructing the grid in itself clarifies both options and objectives.

**Tips**

*Many levels of depth are possible in your analysis. A simple approach would be to simply dot vote which options meet which criteria. Another would be to discuss each link qualitatively and rank 1–5, depending on how well the options meet the criteria.*

*Use the grid as a springboard for discussion. Don't assume the best fit is necessarily the best choice.*

*A voter tool in a web-conference program could be used to evaluate criteria.*

| CRITERIA | 1. option | 2. option | 3. option | 4. option |
|---|---|---|---|---|
| ● | | | | |
| ● | ✓ | ✓ | | |
| ● | | ✓ | | |
| ● | | ✓ | ✓ | |
| ● | | | | ✓ |
| | | | | |

## Steps

1. Identify the different options that need to be decided.

2. List options on sticky notes along the top axis of a large grid.

3. Brainstorm criteria on sticky notes.

4. Arrange them in order of importance along the left side of the grid.

5. Make sure everyone is clear about both options and criteria. Make any changes necessary.

6. Evaluate each option against all the criteria, indicating whether or not it meets the criteria.

7. Discuss which option meets the most criteria.

8. Ask for a decision.

**COMMITMENT**

# Option Analysis

## Use Prioritized Decision Criteria to Assess Multiple Options

Strong disagreements can develop when there are strong advocates for different solutions to the same situation. A helpful way to avoid these polarized positions or break out of them is to first agree on the criteria to be used in making the choice and their relative importance, and then applying these criteria systematically to the options.

**Commitment**

**Time**
2–3 hours

## Tips

*Although this practice is designed to produce objective scores for each option, it is important to remember that the scores are the result of cumulative subjective assessments, and should not be followed slavishly.*

*Don't let a specific option get slipped in as a decision criterion. This would skew the ratings in its favor.*

*This process is based on a more comprehensive process called Decision Analysis described in the classic* The New Rational Manager, *by Charles Kepner.*

| Desirable Criteria | Priority Points | Option A | Rating / Score | Option B | Rating / Score | Option C | Rating / Score |
|---|---|---|---|---|---|---|---|
| Criterion #1 | 40 | ~ | 5 / 200 | ~ | 10 / 400 | ~ | 8 / 320 |
| Criterion #2 | 30 | ~ | 7 / 210 | ~ | 9 / 270 | ~ | 4 / 120 |
| Criterion #3 | 20 | ~ | 3 / 60 | ~ | 6 / 120 | ~ | 7 / 140 |
| Criterion #4 | 10 | ~ | 5 / 50 | ~ | 5 / 50 | ~ | 6 / 60 |
| Total Scores | | | 520 | | 840 | | 640 |

## Steps

1. Identify on sticky notes all relevant criteria that a viable solution needs to satisfy. Separate them into Essential (i.e.—must be fulfilled to be considered viable) and Desirable.

2. Identify all the options being proposed.

3. Eliminate any options that do not satisfy all Essential Criteria or cannot be modified to satisfy these criteria.

4. Prioritize the Desirable Criteria by assigning Priority Points to each criterion such that the points reflect the relative value of that criterion and the total points equal 100.

5. Create a wall matrix in which each row represents a Desirable Criterion and each column represents a Viable Option. Arrange the stickies on the matrix.

6. Establish a rating for how well options satisfy each Desirable Criterion by picking the option that best satisfies that criterion and giving it a 10. Score others based on how they compare to the top-rated option.

7. Calculate an overall score for each option by multiplying its ratings for each criterion by the priority points for that criterion and then adding up these individual criteria scores for a total option score.

8. Compare scores for the options and select the best.

# Assigning Action Items

**Commitment**

**Timing**
During meetings

### Link Tasks to Responsible Parties

During team meetings write down all action items, then assign these items to specific people at the end of the meeting. If done on a copy board, this list provides a copy of commitments and a place to start the following meeting. If not, make sure someone types up the actions and sends them out. If working online, type the list into one of your white-board slides. This practice is a very practical way to build accountability in a team.

**Tips**

*Post the chart at the next meeting to provide an accountability check.*

*Make the Action Items chart as detailed as the team wants.*

## Steps

1. Post an Action Items chart early in a team meeting.

2. Record all action items on this chart whenever they are mentioned in the meeting.

3. Leave a margin on the chart for recording names against items.

4. Publicly assign all items before the meeting ends.

5. Make it clear that one can change his or her assignment, move the date, and so on. Encourage people to note any changes on the master chart so that it can be used for later reference.

**COMMITMENT**

## Commitment

**Time**
10 minutes

# Action Signups

### Get People to Commit Visibly

A tried-and-true way for a group to face the commitment stage is to ask people to sign up for action items at the end of a meeting or retreat. This can be as simple as putting people's names on a list of next steps or as involved as determining champions and action teams for large organizational initiatives. Signing up for action is a critical moment in a group process and requires full leadership involvement. Often in business organizations executives favor assigning people to action items. In community settings it is important to have interested volunteers indicate their commitment.

## Tips

*It helps a team to push a little to make commitments public. This will test consensus if you are working in that mode.*

*Be clear which assignments you want handled by specific people.*

*In teleconferences or web conferences, review the items verbally and get acknowledgement.*

## Steps

1. List potential action items on a chart in front of the room, on a graphic template or in your web-conference program.

2. Explain the importance of having people specifically responsible for the different action items.

3. Ask team members if they want to sign up now, or handle the assignments in some other fashion.

4. Encourage people to call out their name and the item they are signing up for.

5. Write their name next to the item in a way that will show up clearly on the notes.

6. Tell everyone how the minutes or chart documentation will be handled so that they will be looking for their assignment.

# Single-Document Worksheets

**Commitment**

4

**Time**
N/A

## Focus Everyone on One Work Output

A well-tested way to precipitate commitment among parties who have differing views is to use a single document to craft a consensus. A wall template has this effect, as do group worksheets, or a set of draft slides in an online conference. Working together on a single document keeps everyone focused on the shared task, and tracks the changes that are needed to get everyone on board with the new directions. Giving breakout groups a single, large worksheet that spells out what needs to be reported out allows each group to self-organize and still have uniform outputs.

**COMMITMENT**

## Tips

*Design work-sheets so that they have plenty of room in margins and other areas for improvisation.*

*Provide a sample filled out if you need to have the output clear and readable.*

*Use worksheets in advance of a meeting to help key people precipitate their ideas and come prepared.*

## Steps

*1.* Think about the output you want and design a worksheet or template (or pick from standard Grove templates).

*2.* Prepare the number of worksheets you will need for breakout groups.

*3.* Explain the categories on the sheet as you orient people to the process.

*4.* Coach people to feel free to make corrections, write in margins, and even add paper, using the chart as a real worksheet.

*5.* Use Report Backs (page 74) to review the work.

# Supporting Resistance

**Timing**
At the point
of commit-
ment

## Tips

*Before closing a
discussion, ask
for questions,
then say—
"Going once,
going twice,
going a third
time." People
usually laugh
but it makes the
point.*

*Leaders who
push commit-
ment on their
teams can
undermine
progress.*

*This is one stage
where it is
important to "go
slow to go fast"
later.*

*If the whole
group becomes
resistant, refer to
the charter and
ask—"What is
our central pur-
pose here?" That
usually gets
things going
again.*

### Let the Group Make the Turn

Teams need everyone's commitment to truly turn the corner to effective implementation. In work, as in mountain climbing, stragglers control the climb. Work with this phenomenon and support minority viewpoints. Encourage resisters to fully express themselves. Dealing with doubts will only strengthen the clarity of the team's commitment. If new information challenges plans, celebrate the resources and time you save by finding out early. Online, you will need to specifically call on people and draw out comments from those you know have issues.

## Steps

1. Orient yourself to the value of single voices and skeptics raising important issues.

2. As the team gains in commitment, support these minority positions' expressing themselves.

3. Keep an Issues chart going during commitment meetings, and specifically deal with each issue.

4. Let the team's members themselves respond to doubters. As a leader, support all individual viewpoints being heard.

5. Check all commitments and agreements to see if there are any questions or final comments before closing.

# Dot Voting

## *Show Group Interest Graphically*

**Commitment**

**Time**

15 minutes

Multicolored sticky dots provide a fast and graphic way to poll group interest and sort data into priorities. Online programs provide white-board markers that make a nice dot. Any kind of graphic display can be evaluated in this fashion by giving people a set of dots, explaining what the colors mean, and asking people to dot the specific pieces of information on the display. The process gets everyone up and actively reviewing the work. Online, the dots popping into the display is fun. The result is a visual footprint of people's interest, capable of being scanned rapidly for centers of interest. The dots can also be counted and tallied in a more analytical fashion if you wish.

## Tips

*Instruct people to put dots in the same place for each item—i.e. to the left, under, to the right, and so on.*

*Number items for easy reference.*

*Keep your color system and number of dots simple, so that attention is on the evaluation and not on the mechanics.*

*Avery brand dots are available in most stationery stores in a full range of sizes and colors.*

*Dot voting does evoke some peer pressure, which may or may not be useful in reaching agreement.*

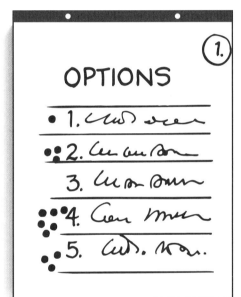

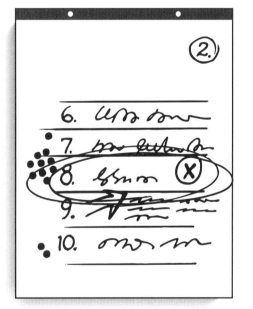

**COMMITMENT**

## Steps

1. Record items that you wish to evaluate on flip charts or large displays, leaving space for the dots to be added later.

2. Estimate how many dots each person should have. The main limitation is space on the display.

3. Color code dots for more information—e.g. red equals top priority, yellow means needs development, and so forth.

4. Ask everyone to approach the display and place their dots.

5. Stand back and conduct a discussion about what the dots tell you.

6. Record conclusions on a separate chart.

# Multi-Voting

**Commitment**

**Time**
2 hours

### *Evaluate Group-wide Interest*

Get a sense of how your team as a whole evaluates the importance of goals by taking a nonbinding vote on multiple ideas. Ask team members to select their top one-third of the items —framing the activity as a mirror of group priorities and a springboard for decisions, not as a win/lose vote. This practice can be seen as a type of group poll to test priorities. The value of multi-voting is in people making their rating without peer pressure. Online, people can check items on a slide with their cursors.

**Tips**
*Use slashes or another color to differentiate votes from the item number.*

*Keep the discussion periods open and lively.*

*Do not assume everyone agrees on goals. After you take the poll, expect further discussion.*

## Steps

1. List goals or action proposals.

2. Discuss each for clarity and understanding.

3. Combine similar items if necessary.

4. Number the items; allow each person to vote for one-third of the list.

5. Indicate action by hand vote and tally on the chart.

6. Discuss the poll for insights about practices.

# Chartering

**Commitment**

**Time**
30–45 minutes

## Be Clear About What Is Expected from Teams

"Chartering" may be the most important thing to do well with a team, especially as it moves to action. A minimal charter would include a summary of goals and a set of deadlines. The charter may have been shared in the initial stages of team development, but in Stage 4 of the TPM it needs to be reclarified. Make sure that agreements on constraints, budgetary and otherwise, are included and that deliverables are clearly identified. A charter works best when it is written out clearly so that the team can refer back to it as work progresses.

**Tips**
*If a team is self chartering, encourage them to check out their assumptions with whoever is needed for sponsorship.*

*This practice is a good way to create temporary task forces or coordinating committees.*

## Steps

1. When a team has been assigned to complete a task, suggest that an explicit charter be created.

2. Begin by clarifying the goals of the team.

3. Identify any deadlines.

4. Characterize what the deliverable or results should look like in as explicit terms as possible.

5. Draw out ideas about who should be on the team and who should lead it, if these decisions are not already settled.

6. Identify other constraints.

7. Give a copy of the charter to the team leader or convener.

**COMMITMENT**

# Committing the Organization

**Commitment**

**Timing**
Days

## Create a Reliable Platform for Group Work

At the commitment stage of team development, to be truly effective a team needs organizational commitments that are as firm as its own sense of direction. This is especially true of inter-departmental, cross-divisional and other cross-boundary teams. When facilitating action plans for teams, make sure you spend time thinking through how the team will get this commitment if they do not have it already. Sharing plans and getting ownership from sponsors is an important way to accomplish this. For virtual teams, supplying a shared infrastructure and schedule of meetings becomes essential.

**Tips**

*There are no formulas or recipes for getting commitment from the larger organization. This is a practice that requires attention to the real, unique conditions present in each situation.*

*If organizational commitments are conditional, or weak, this doesn't mean the team cannot function. But it helps to know this in advance and avoid false expectations.*

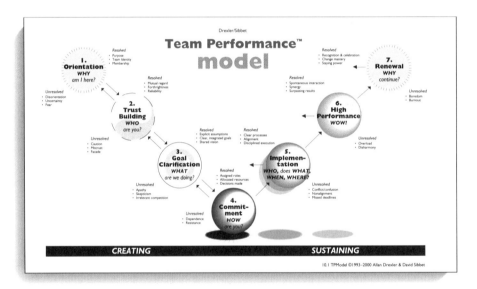

## Steps

1.  Clarify the organization resources and support that will be needed to achieve the team's goals.

2.  Confer with your team sponsors and determine whether they are willing to provide the necessary organizational commitments.

3.  Clarify details about the organizational commitments during action planning.

4.  If commitments are too vague or inadequate, draw out ideas from the team about how to engage the organization.

5.  Engage the team's formal sponsor as an advocate in securing the commitments needed.

# Three-Party Contracting

### Resolve Dual-Reporting Conflicts

Commitment requires clarity of goals and roles. In situations where team members report to both a team leader and a functional boss, hold a three-way meeting to be clear about roles and responsibilities and to make agreements about how to handle potential conflicts. Making trade-offs without explicit agreements leaves a team member in the middle with accompanying tensions and loss of effectiveness. Agreements prevent many unintended difficulties.

**Commitment**

**Time**
2 hours

## Tips
*The key to this kind of negotiation is getting information out before you try to make any decisions.*

*Assume each party is working to achieve what it thinks is best for the organization.*

*In a high-conflict situation invite a neutral party to help facilitate a resolution.*

*It is often facilitative for the two bosses to talk first to establish their ground rules.*

## Steps

*1.* Contact each party involved and identify areas of conflict.

*2.* Schedule a three-way meeting to explore a possible win/win situation.

*3.* Come prepared to lay out your needs and your recommendation for a solution, if you can think of one. Ask each person to prepare similarly.

*4.* If there is a problem in getting an easy resolution, have each party make a list of what they need and what they are willing to give to make the situation work.

*5.* Compare the lists and identify areas of agreement.

*6.* Search for solutions that address the critical needs of each party.

COMMITMENT

## Role Alignment

**Time**
2 hours

### *Publicly Agree on Roles*

Public agreements about roles and responsibilities operate like contracts. They make things clear for team members and help release energy for commitment and implementation. This practice outlines a way to do this on charts where everyone lists their own responsibilities and can also respond to others' lists. The process is designed to maximize communication and minimize conflict. Virtual teams would need to have people prepare these lists in advance, then initial them with cursors.

**Tips**

*The value of this activity stems from the fact that most role confusion comes from unclear or missing communication.*

*Be prepared to deal with conflicts.*

*If a disagreement involves only a couple of people, let them handle it on their own time without involving the whole group.*

*Make a list of all the conflict items that need attention.*

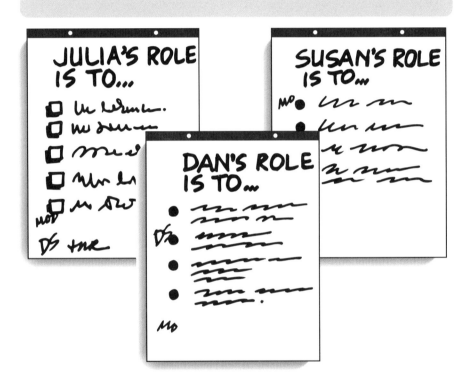

## Steps

1. Orient everyone to the purpose of the activity.

2. Ask members to create a chart with their names on top, listing first the responsibilities involved in their role and then any questions they have about their responsibilities.

3. Invite everyone to read each other's lists and initial any item that they feel needs to be clarified.

4. As a team, review each chart and discuss each marked item and question that remains unanswered.

5. Clear up misunderstandings, address missing items, and identify sticky issues that need further work to resolve.

6. Agree on appropriate steps to address unresolved issues.

# Responsibility Charting

**Commitment**

**Time**
1–2 hours

## Confront Boundary Issues

The most comprehensive way to clarify roles and commit to responsibilities is for the team to create a chart matching team members on one side with team tasks on the other. In the grid indicate the various types of responsibilities people have. Indicate direct responsibility (R), approval authority (A), support responsibility (S), and responsibility to stay informed (I). The process of creating the matrix and filling it out has great value in helping a team understand its organizational structure and contract a turn toward high performance.

**Tips**

*Clearly define each responsibility so that there is complete agreement about what R, A, S, and I mean (no fuzzy definitions).*

*Be prepared for an intense and often long session.*

*Let the group take time to discuss any issues that seem sensitive.*

*Document this work and have it on reference as a living contract.*

*An alternative to the "RASI" letters is to use colored dots or different shapes.*

**TEAM** **TASKS**

| | | | | | |
|---|---|---|---|---|---|
| • Geoff | R | A | A | R | I | I |
| • Judy | I | R | I | A | | |
| • Stan | S | S | R | | A | A |
| • Jesse | S | I | I | I | R | R |
| • Hillary | | I | S | S | S | S |

## Steps

1. Hang a large sheet of paper on the wall.

2. Create a large grid or matrix with markers; title it.

3. List names of all members down the left side.

4. Ask the group to identify all key tasks of the team and list them along the top.

5. Check the group to see if the four types of responsibilities listed above are the most important. Add others as needed.

6. Use the "RASI" letters to go over each task and individualize the type of responsibility the person has. Have people fill out the matrix individually. Then fill in the master matrix, work out differences, and keep a list of all issues that are raised.

**COMMITMENT**

# Creating Portfolios

**Time**
2 hours

## Link Resources with Plans for Customer Targets

Services and products follow a life cycle not unlike living systems. Once you have identified target markets, use a "sow, grow, harvest and plow" framework to see where you stand with each product or service you intend to offer. This way resources can be allocated more effectively. Set the criteria for where each product and service should fall in the cycle by referring to priority objectives. This disciplines your team to be conscious about what "crops" it is supporting. The final portfolio decisions should always be guided by your vision of who your customers are.

**Tips**

*Be prepared for a challenging session. This practice demands a lot of clarity and agreement.*

*This practice should be followed by action planning and phasing of work.*

*Identify trade-offs. Further research may be needed to complete the portfolio.*

### Investment Portfolio Graphic Guide®

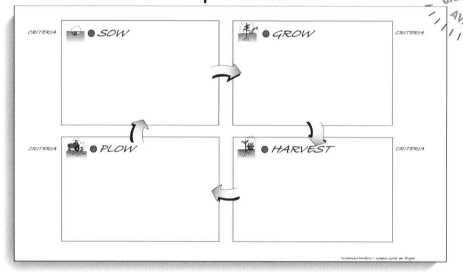

## Steps

1. Post a large 2x2 matrix with the headings shown above, use The Grove's Investment Portfolio Graphic Guide®, or create a white-board template online.

2. Identify all products and services on sticky notes or cards.

3. Discuss the criteria for each quadrant, using the vision or business plan as a reference.

4. Place the product and service cards in the appropriate quadrant.

5. Analyze the chart for balance and focus.

6. Make decisions about balance and overall work load.

See the *Investment Portfolio Leader's Guide* for detailed instructions on how to use this Graphic Guide (www.grove.com).

# Graphic Gameplan

## Align Teams to the Big Picture

Teams need a big picture to guide their work together just as a sports team needs an overarching game strategy to direct its play. This practice summarizes, in one graphic display, key understandings needed to begin work. By integrating a portrait of the team with a clear statement of results, major phases and tasks of the work—together with critical success factors and challenges—members have an opportunity to see where they are going.

**Commitment**

**Time**
1–3 hours

## Tips

*If team goals are unclear or leadership issues are unresolved, they should be addressed first.*

*Encourage people to share what they do know and not get stuck on what is missing.*

*Gain 100 percent participation to ensure commitment.*

### Graphic Gameplan Graphic Guide®

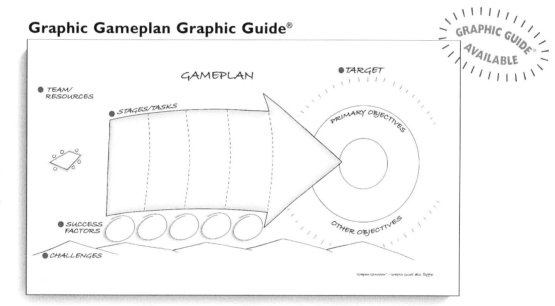

COMMITMENT

## Steps

1. Orient the team to the purpose of the Graphic Gameplan Graphic Guide.

2. Introduce the team; describe skills, resources, and so on.

3. Clarify overall results and objectives, including personal objectives.

4. List big phases of the project; let the headings tell a story; brainstorm tasks under stages.

5. Brainstorm key tasks in each phase. Use sticky notes or list.

6. Identify critical success factors or guiding principles.

7. Identify challenges to overcome.

8. Commit to redrafting and posting the gameplan.

See the *Graphic Gameplan Leader's Guide* for detailed instructions on how to use this Graphic Guide (www.grove.com).

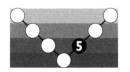

# 5. Implementation Stage

## *Who Does What, When and Where?*

Implementation engages a team in scheduling and sequencing activities, and solving problems as they arise. Action brings flexibility and a bit of uncertainty back into your work, as well as the excitement of making progress. Your team can track its work against plans so that all team members and decision makers can stay aligned and make necessary adjustments.

### Supporting Execution

After committing to a direction, team members need to get to work and take action. The practices here support being clear about who is to do what, as well as methods for supporting accountability and follow-through.

### Clarifying Processes

People perform tasks more effectively when they are clear about the process they are using. Practices in this section will help you create explicit action plans and gameplans that show timing, milestones, and who is responsible for what. Graphic communications are very helpful at this stage.

### Staying Aligned

When everyone consistently pulls in the same direction toward the same goals, attention can focus on the challenges of getting there. Non-alignment soaks up a lot of resources and time. Best practices here involve holding review meetings and check-ins that allow you to make adjustments in the day-to-day work and still maintain an overall direction that remains constant.

**IMPLEMENTATION**

LET'S HIT THAT RAMP STRAIGHT ON!

# IMPLEMENTATION PRACTICES

# Next Steps

**Time**
15–30 minutes

## End Meetings by Linking to Action

Make sure meetings and processes are linked by ending each one with a Next Steps session. A simple approach involves putting up a chart and listing everyone's suggestions, then going back and making assignments and creating deadlines. A more involved approach would involve preparing a chart of the upcoming process and reviewing it with the group. This is a good time to check overall gameplans and outcomes lists. Online, end your your session with a review of suggested actions.

## Tips

*Even if you have agenda items left to consider, stop soon enough to hold a Next Steps session.*

*Public sign-up for tasks strengthens the commitment of the person(s) undertaking the assignments.*

## Steps

1. Label a flip chart Next Steps.

2. Review any "parking lot" charts or "bins" where you have been storing action items.

3. Create a list of all identified next steps.

4. Ask for names and times and write them on the chart.

5. Double-check to make sure all items are listed.

6. Distribute the list to all participants after the meeting.

**IMPLEMENTATION**

# To-Do Lists

**Timing**
N/A

### *Keep a Rolling Update*

For working groups, a To-Do list is a convenient way to manage implementation. A simple list keeps track of whatever your group needs to do. A more developed list might include the action item, persons responsible, and date due. Some teams keep a list like this on an electronic spreadsheet and start meetings by reviewing what has been accomplished and updating deadlines. During meetings it is good practice to keep a To-Do list on a flip chart for any action items that need follow-up.

## Tips
*List one action per item.*

*Record the name of the person(s) responsible for each item.*

*Use an electronic spreadsheet for more complicated projects or a project management program that generates To-Do lists as one of its tools.*

## Steps

1. Record action items on a chart during meetings or in the white board of a web-conference program.

2. Write up the items in a To-Do list after the meeting.

3. Use the list as a start for the next meeting, to check against actions.

# Kickoffs

## Use Face-to-Face to Support Virtual Work

Kickoffs are used when a team moves to implementation and involves a wide range of people. These meetings help to clarify goals and provide a space for buy-in and trust building. With people using remote communications more frequently, it is even more important to have high quality, face-to-face kickoffs for key projects. People will be more likely to trust those they have met personally. More focused communications are common in implementation. They work better if everyone has some shared background and understandings. Kickoffs also ensure that everyone gets a chance to clear up confusions about direction and goals. They provide a setting in which to sort out roles and other organizational issues before getting to work.

## Tips

*Organization-wide kickoffs can involve a lot of celebration in a "rally" atmosphere. They provide a chance to celebrate past achievements as you get ready to tackle new challenges.*

*Teams can hold kickoff meetings online using Web-conferencing programs or teleconferencing. Provide plenty of time for introductions and questions because the pace is slower and there is no equivalent of breaks and free time for people to get to know each other.*

## Steps

*1.* Plan a formal kickoff at the start of important projects.

*2.* If a large number of participants is involved, use a process design team (see Process Design Meetings, page 53) to get increased participation.

*3.* Arrange for senior leadership to present key visions and plans.

*4.* Create overview murals and other presentations that give everyone a common, big picture.

*5.* Plan for breakouts, discussions, and town hall meetings that allow people to thoroughly understand what is expected.

*6.* Ground communications about plans in action-plan work sessions.

*7.* Have people leave with clear assignments.

**IMPLEMENTATION**

# Web and Teleconferences

**Time**
1–1.5 hours

## Tips

*Say your name to identify yourself before speaking.*

*Clearly identify the titles of any documents you are referencing.*

*Review for understanding before deciding.*

*If you need to leave the conference, let everyone know before signing off.*

*Use a shared target template or document, either hard copy or soft, to focus the teleconference.*

*For big group decisions, hold a series of conferences using a small group in between to create draft decisions or proposals.*

## Coordinate Electronically in Real Time

Web conferences and teleconferences are common ways that working teams communicate and stay aligned. They are similar in that you set up a call log-in. Web conferencing includes viewing a shared computer screen. Web and teleconferences are important when people need to work through tricky issues that will benefit from the back-and-forth exchanges where people can build on each other's ideas. They work best for providing broad input from everyone, and having everyone hear the same thing in regard to plans and directions. The medium is more challenging for making decisions and coming to closure on topics.

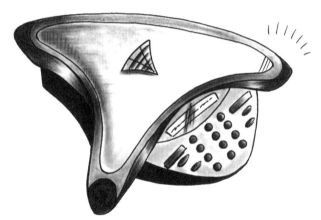

## Steps

1. Schedule the meeting with a web or teleconference service.

2. E-mail, voice-mail or fax a meeting agenda, URL, password, background material and target documents in advance.

3. When hosting, check into the conference at least five minutes early and keep a list of who is logging on.

4. When everyone is present, lead a go-around for introductions. Review the agenda and basic ground rules for participation.

5. Facilitate the teleconference by clearly announcing agenda topics, reinforcing basic ground rules and summarizing exchanges.

6. Provide brief updates for anyone checking in late.

7. Close the conference with a review of action items. Send out minutes of the conference soon after it is over.

# Early Wins

## *Succeed one Step at a Time*

Early in implementation, encourage your team to solve small problems and experience regular, small wins. Make sure these are noticed by others. This practice is especially important for new teams or disempowered teams. The habit of success builds like muscles and needs to be established through regular, small victories. E-mail acknowledgements, updates, and group voice-mails are ways to celebrate with virtual teams.

**Implementation**

**Time**
2 hours

**Tips**

*Select something small enough to complete and improve.*

*Small wins give teams courage to take on bigger challenges.*

*Select problems that people have a strong interest in addressing.*

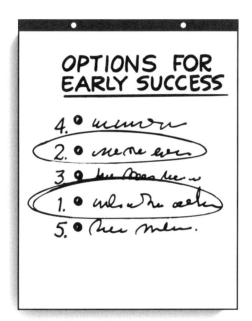

## Steps

1. Create charts summarizing small problems the team might solve.

2. Ask the team to rank the problems from most likely to get a win to least likely.

3. Collect data on the problem.

4. Decide how to address the findings.

5. Take action.

6. Evaluate the improvement.

IMPLEMENTATION

# Gameplan Posters

Implementation

**Timing**
Keep on
display

### Reinforce the Big Picture

When a group has gone to the trouble to create an action plan or gameplan, create a cleaned-up version and post it permanently in the team room or meeting room during meetings, or create a special slide for web conferences. This visual will automatically help members keep the big picture in mind during all the real-life twists and turns. If significant changes occur, then the group will challenge the accuracy of the plan and you can decide if you need to update it or move on.

**Tips**
*Adding graphics to the gameplan helps with memorability.*

*Dry chalk pastels can add color that looks like an airbrush. Rub color onto a tissue, and then add the color to the chart. Oil pastels don't work as well.*

*Make sure the size fits the space available for posting. A small version could be color copied and placed in individual cubicles.*

**Graphic Gameplan Graphic Guide®**

*GRAPHIC GUIDE® AVAILABLE*

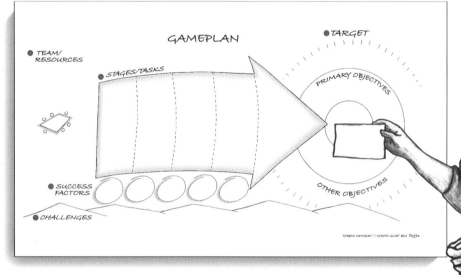

## Steps

1. Use The Grove's Graphic Gameplan Graphic Guide or have someone draw whatever gameplan the group is using, or translate the poster to a PowerPoint® slide using The Grove's digital templates.

2. Bring this graphic to the group for review and editing. This deepens understanding of the plan.

3. Create a final version and post for reference.

# Gantt Charting

### Agree on Tasks, Milestones and Deliverables

Charting tasks against time and milestones in a Gantt Chart is one of the most widely practiced ways of planning a project. Tasks are usually listed down the left side, while time is listed across the top. Bars mark the amount of time the task will take and diamonds or "X's" mark the deadlines. Milestones and decision points are also indicated. Many computer programs support this kind of charting. The process your team goes through in completing this chart is critical to team commitment. Maintaining and updating the chart supports implementation.

**Implementation**

**Time**
2 hours

## Tips

*Use this activity after a Graphic Gameplan session (page 128).*

*Use sticky notes to identify and sort tasks if you want to order order them in a particular way.*

*Keep to a standard level of detail. Major tasks may need a second Gantt Chart breaking out the subtasks.*

*Sometimes there is value in having subteams work on parts. Then, bringing it back to a planning session ties it together.*

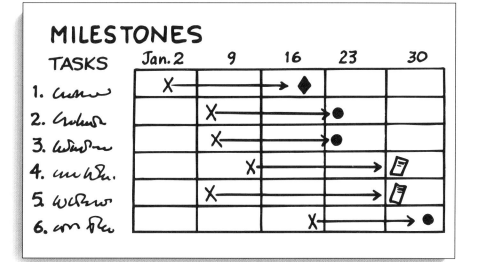

## Steps

1. Create a large grid on an electronic white board or chart paper.

2. List all tasks down the left-hand side of the chart; place times across the top for total length of the project.

3. Mark the likely starting point and ending point of each task, then draw a horizontal bar between the points.

4. Use a standard graphic symbol to indicate deliverables (such as a diamond or square for a document); place these on the bars where they occur.

5. Transfer to a computer spreadsheet, project management program or art program for later reference and updating.

6. Display this large chart in the team's workspace.

**IMPLEMENTATION**

**Implementation**

**Time**
2 hours

# Process Maps

## *Visualize the Work Flow from the Top Down*

Graphic flow charts or "process maps" provide a high-level perspective on the entire team process. Using consistent and intuitively clear graphic symbols makes the practice even more powerful. Circles for meetings, squares for output documents and arrows for projects, all linked on a timeline, create a visual that works like a road for a traveler. Objectives and milestones can be added easily to such a display.

## Tips

*Break long processes into four or five stages and give them memorable names along the top of the map.*

*Color code the meetings if that kind of differentiation makes the map easier to read.*

*When reproducing for distribution, include a conventional Milestones memo or list agenda.*

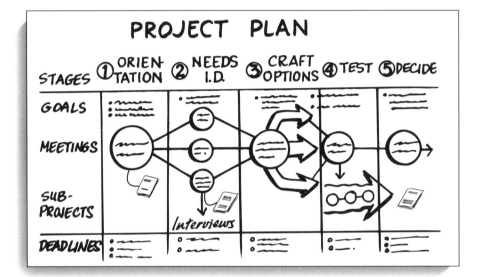

## Steps

1. Locate agendas, Gantt Charts and other documents showing tasks or workplans.

2. Outline a timeline running left to right on a large chart.

3. Map all critical meetings as circles, showing bigger meetings as larger circles.

4. Map all output documents as little document icons.

5. Show mini projects as arrows.

6. Put oversight activities toward the top, support operations along the bottom.

7. List each meeting's name, objectives and milestones as words around the graphic map.

# Progress Charting

**Timing**
Ongoing

## Show Accomplishments So That All Can See

Feedback on results is essential for teams to stay motivated and focused during execution times. Fundraising projects use thermometer graphics to chart their progress. An engineering manager regularly passes out a graphic workplan with results highlighted in yellow. Factories sometimes have tote boards that click off whenever products pass inspection. Virtual teams might check in on web conferences and review a set of progress slides. The key in this practice is to visualize progress in whatever fashion your situation allows.

### Tips

*Get the team involved in making the progress report.*

*Keep it simple.*

*Link acknowledgements and celebrations to progress.*

### Steps

1. Decide which measures are the most important indicators of progress.

2. Plan a way to easily take these measures and assign responsibility.

3. Create a poster or display in a prominent place at work.

4. Assign a person to regularly log the measures on the display.

5. Reference the progress report in project review meetings.

**IMPLEMENTATION**

# Objectives Reviews

**Implementation**

**Time**
2 hours

**Tips**

*Creating an environment where people are willing to explore difficulties they are encountering requires good management and a shared belief in the power of collaboration. It may require strong encouragement to get people to open up. Achieving this kind of openness can do more for the results a team will achieve than anything else you might do.*

*Think about whether or not you need to support the team in some trust building practices to set the proper climate for effective objectives reviews.*

## Focus on Progress Against Goals

Implementation for task-oriented teams is well supported by regular objectives reviews. These meetings focus on progress toward goals. An effective objectives review asks everyone what is being accomplished and what is getting in the way of progress. Best practice would involve inviting people to be clear about where they are running into difficulty and to help each other eliminate barriers. It helps to have the group focus on a large calendar showing progress on a three-month road map. It isn't helpful to go out much further than this for regular reviews.

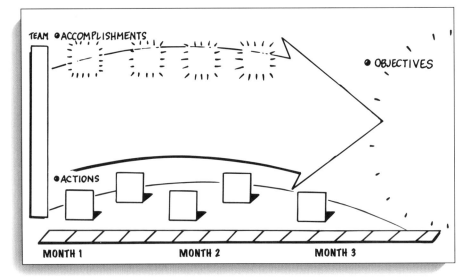

## Steps

1. Prepare a large, three-month calendar with the overall objectives clearly indicated.

2. Ask each person to report on progress.

3. Record what has been accomplished.

4. Identify where people are encountering difficulty meeting deadlines and commitments.

5. Brainstorm how the team can support them in removing barriers and making progress.

6. Keep the focus to three months.

7. Record new commitments.

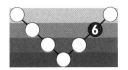

# 6. High Performance Stage

## *Getting to WOW!*

All of the investment your team has made in the prior stages really pays off when it reaches full momentum in sustained alignment and commitment. This comes from mastering processes and transcending the need to have everything spelled out in detail. This stage is challenging to sustain, but can happen regularly with practice.

### Surpassing Results

High performance is marked by an ability not only to achieve goals but also to surpass them or refocus them as conditions change. These practices focus on the kinds of reviews and feedback needed to continually improve processes and the quality of participation.

### Deepening Synergy

Synergy means accomplishing something much greater as a whole than individuals working separately could accomplish. When talents mesh and people collaborate across cultures and geographies, amazing things can be achieved. This requires a deep sense of trust and loyalty that can be nurtured. The practices that foster group-wide learning and engagement are clustered here.

WE'RE FLYING WITH THESE PRACTICES

HIGH PERFORMANCE

# HIGH PERFORMANCE PRACTICES

# Meeting Evaluations

## Find Out What Worked

Taking some time at the end of a face-to-face or virtual meeting or project to find out what worked and what could improve is one of the most effective ways of improving performance capability in a group. Contract to spend 10 minutes at the end of a meeting to hear from everyone. Write all ideas on a chart. Encourage everyone to express individual ideas, without discussion or evaluation.

**High Performance**

**Time**
10–15 minutes

## Tips

*To start the "to improve" segment, say, "Imagine leaving this meeting and telling a friend about it—what would you complain about?"*

*If the group resists, argue for the value of dealing with issues before they spread. The value of this practice far outweighs any discomfort it may involve.*

**WHAT WORKED?**

+ Everyone participating
+ Facilitation
+ Right people
+ Good planning
+ Bob's presentation

**WHAT COULD IMPROVE?**

→ People coming on time
→ More discussion on roles
→ Room with windows
→ Longer

## Steps

1. Include time for evaluation in meeting agendas.

2. Draw a "T" bar on a big chart, use two flip pads, or use your online white board. Label the left pad "What worked" and the right "What to improve."

3. Encourage people to share their personal opinions, starting with "what worked."

4. Summarize all comments on the chart using the person's own needs when possible.

5. Make sure all problems are brought up in the group rather than in the hall.

6. Acknowledge each contribution without evaluation. Just say, "thank you," "got it," or "OK."

**HIGH PERFORMANCE**

**High
Performance**

**Time**
2 hours

# Strengths/Weaknesses Review

## *Take Time to Reflect*

All teams benefit from taking stock of their strengths and weaknesses periodically in order to understand why they succeeded and how they can improve their work together. This practice structures an opportunity for individuals to assess their own strengths and weaknesses in relation to immediate team/organizational goals as well as to identify their preference for personal skill development. Its purpose is to make people feel supported rather than criticized.

### Tips
*Coach the group to see weaknesses as opportunities (use an arrow instead of a "minus" to imply progress not deficiency).*

*This practice works well at the end of a task meeting or project.*

*Begin with noting accomplishments of the team and acknowledging strengths as successes.*

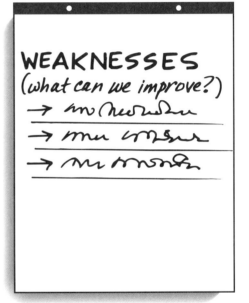

## Steps

*1.* Explain that evaluations are key to performance improvement and better done as a team than "in the hall."

*2.* Begin with strengths—what works now.

*3.* Continue with weaknesses—what can be improved.

*4.* Encourage full discussion.

*5.* Make action assignments on weaknesses if need be.

# Pop-Up Sessions

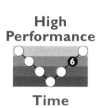
## Take Quick Time-Outs to Learn and Adjust

High performance teams "pop up" from the action now and then to take stock, reconnect with the big picture, and change direction and procedures as needed. This practice ensures that your team stays flexible, learns as it goes and keeps everyone involved. There are many ways of conducting such sessions, but making them snappy, focused and oriented toward results works best for busy teams. Virtual teams might have a quick teleconference.

### Tips
*Vary the format of pop-ups so they do not become routine or boring.*

*Encourage participation in making the meetings fresh and stimulating.*

*Make sure to feed back results.*

*Use basic practices from this guide to conduct your meetings.*

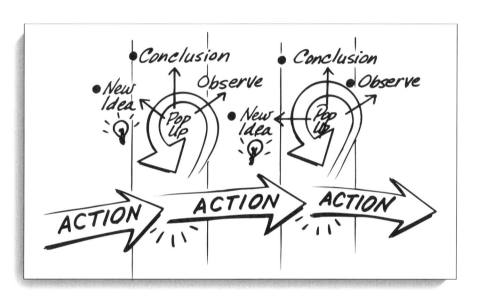

## Steps

1. Explain the value of periodic pop-up sessions to enhance flexibility and communications.

2. Stay on top of the time. Focus on specific items that seem to need attention.

3. Establish a climate where any perspective is valued.

4. Keep a group memory.

5. Plan some pop-ups that allow a general discussion and reconnecting with basic purposes.

**HIGH PERFORMANCE**

## High Performance

**Time**

1–2 hours

**Tips**

*Your role in this process is to facilitate the team members solving the problem rather than solving it for them.*

*Ask relevant questions rather than supplying answers.*

*If underperformance by a specific team member becomes an issue, focus this process on overcoming the performance gap through collective effort of the team. Address the performance issue directly with the team member separately.*

*Use slides and the chat function on web conferences to gather ideas.*

# Team-Based Problem Solving

## *Mobilize the Team's Collective Abilities to Address a Team Performance Issue*

Performance problems often result from multiple factors rather than a single cause. Resolving them may require the combined knowledge and skills of the whole team. Success at resolving the problems can strengthen the team.

### Mandala Chart

## Steps

1. Set up a problem-solving session with the team to address the performance concern.

2. State the problem in relation to the relevant performance expectations and the importance of achieving these expectations. Avoid making blaming statements.

3. Enlist team members in pooling their experience and skills to find the best way to resolve the problem.

4. Facilitate an open problem-solving session to:

   —explore likely causes and contributing factors;
   —brainstorm a full range of possible solutions and options for limiting the impact of the problem;
   —agree on a specific course of action with specific responsbilities and timelines;
   —establish a clear process for follow-up.

5. Facilitate a "lessons learned" session once the problem has been handled.

# Team Performance Progress Reviews

## Review Progress Toward Major Objectives to Manage Attention and Focus

A formal Progress Review focuses the team's energy and attention toward the achievement of important goals and objectives. Delegated accountabilities are both reinforced and supported through this formalized review of progress, and variances are addressed in a timely manner.

## Tips

*Coach those reporting progress on how to present crisp, focused reports.*

*Fine-tune the initial Progress Review meetings by facilitating a "what worked, what could improve" review of the meetings themselves (See Meeting Evaluations, page 135).*

*Balance the time demands for virtual teams so no one group consistently has awkward times.*

**→ KEY OBJECTIVE**

| | |
|---|---|
| Current Progress: | Compatibility testing completed |
| Key Variances: | 3 conflicts with systems identified |
| Causes: | Coding protocols difficult to translate |
| Actions Taken: | Translation sub-system specified |
| Decisions Needed: | Allocation of additional programming resources |

## Steps

1. Schedule regular meetings to report on progress against major objectives, either face-to-face or online.

2. Ask members to report on progress toward objectives by summarizing:

   —actual performance to date;
   —variances from objectives;
   —causes of variances;
   —actions taken to correct negative variances or capitalize on positive ones;
   —any recommendations requiring decisions.

3. Invite other members to offer support and address problems that require their input or decisions.

4. Summarize decisions made and agreed-to actions.

**HIGH PERFORMANCE**

**High
Performance**

**Time**
2–5 hours

## Tips

*Identify logical channels for work using functions or project teams, for instance.*

*Use Dot Voting (page 111) or sticky notes to identify disconnects or strengths once your diagram is complete.*

*Use blank cards to correct labels. This process cycles back a lot as people add or remove detail, so work with a large space.*

*Use color-coded cards to make the display easier to read.*

*Create a "should" map of preferred states with the same process.*

# Work Flow Diagrams

## *Map Current and Preferred States*

A powerful way to understand and improve basic organizational processes is to diagram them on a large chart with a group. If you use large cards (5" by 8" or larger) and tape, you create elements for all decision points and task functions in a work process, and then connect them in the sequence in which they occur. The art in this process is keeping the discussion at a high enough level to be manageable, and at a specific enough level to be meaningful. Illustrate the work flow in whatever way is clear to the group making the diagram. Be creative.

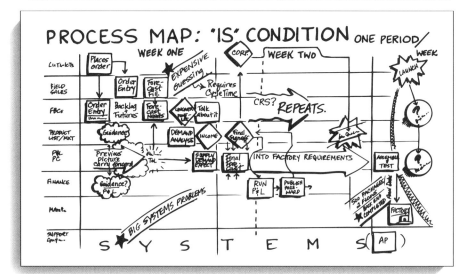

## Steps

*1.* Sit down with some people before a work flow meeting to create a draft diagram of the process with small sticky notes.

*2.* Decide at what level of detail you want to work. Begin the session by posting a large piece of paper.

*3.* Plot the high-level stages of the process on the chart (drawn from your pre-work).

*4.* Generate individual cards or big sticky notes for each critical decision point and each task step.

*5.* Tape the cards in proper sequence on the display. Draw work flow lines when you get agreement.

*6.* Use separate colors to draw feedback loops. Use the diagram to identify issues, strengths, disconnections, and opportunities.

*7.* In designing the work flow, look for opportunities to simplify and streamline the process.

# Customer Visits

## Appreciate Your Stakeholders' Perspective

Have your team spend specific time role playing situations from their customers' point of view to build appreciation of that perspective. An even more concrete way is to interview your customers at their site about their business. Virtual teams can hold web conferences with customers. One company conducted video interviews with customers and required that the entire management participate in making the edits for a final video on company values. Whatever it takes, practice taking a customer view so that you can move to it whenever you need that perspective.

## Tips

*Japanese firms pioneered creating a "House of Quality" that compares a company's criteria of quality against their customers' criteria. The resulting tables are considered the "crown jewels" of a cutomer-oriented business.*

*Just ask — "How would our customers look at this?"*

## Steps

1. Identify the key customers for your team.

2. Think about repeating situations that you could ask the team to role play.

3. Write out the situations on slips of paper, one slip per role, telling what the person in that role wants from an exchange.

4. Have pairs play out the roles.

5. Discuss insights generated about the customer.

6. Identify the critical characteristics of your customers' perspective.

**HIGH PERFORMANCE**

**High Performance**

**Time**

1–2 hours

## Tips

*Both parties may place you in the position of agreeing with their point of view and imposing their preferred resolution on the other party. Your task is to help them jointly find an acceptable resolution.*

*What is often missing in these situations is some shared appreciation for what value each person brings to the team. As team leader you can ask them to share unacknowledged appreciations with each other.*

*It is useful to discuss and agree on conflict mediation processes during team startup meetings so everyone has the same information and expectations.*

# Conflict Mediation

## *Address Issues Between Team Members Before They Cripple Team Effectiveness*

Disagreements of both substance and style can grow into major disruptions if they are not resolved. As team leader you need to insist that the issues be addressed and provide a process of engagement aimed at producing agreements that both parties can accept.

## Steps

1. Meet with all parties separately to understand their perspectives and then propose a process for jointly resolving the issues.

2. Convene the parties at a time and place where everyone can meet without interruption, either face-to-face or online.

3. Ask all parties to describe their own needs and interests and what they think are the needs and interests of the other parties. Coach them to do this without blaming or attacking each other.

4. If any party seems locked into a fixed position, encourage them to describe what needs lie behind that position.

5. Separate the needs into those that the parties share, those that are simply different, and those that are in fundamental opposition.

6. Ask the parties to identify opportunities to support each other in the first two categories, and ways they might compromise in the last category.

7. Propose a resolution based on the ideas suggested and test for agreement.

8. Establish clear steps and responsibilities for all follow-up actions.

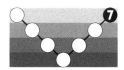

# 7. Renewal Stage

## *Why Continue?*

Teams enter the renewal stage when they finish projects, experience large organizational changes, undergo policy shifts, or even take on new members. Change necessitates new responses. Renewal is essential for fast-paced work that can burn people out. Investing in renewal also creates real dividends when new teams form and can bring forward learning and insight from prior experiences.

### Building Staying Power
True staying power comes from keeping everyone involved, refocusing commitment to vision and goals, and providing time to deal with issues that build up.

### Recognizing and Celebrating
Being seen and appreciated makes a huge difference in people's sense of accomplishment. Recognition and sharing of best practices is also a key to building overall organizational capability long term. Practices grouped here help you with critical removal points and true endings.

RENEWAL

# RENEWAL
# PRACTICES

# Back on Board

**Renewal**

**Time**
2 hours

## Remotivate Burned-Out Teams

For teams that have lost motivation, ask everyone to create a sticky note answering the question "What would get me back on board?" Post these and then discuss them one by one. Sometimes people get discouraged because the relentless pace of events provides no time to express concerns or adjust expectations. This practice creates a space to address these issues and allows people a positive context for making adjustments.

## Tips
*Facing issues directly takes away their hidden power and makes it possible to move again.*

*Don't be surprised if good ideas emerge. The flip side of every perceived problem is a vision of something being different.*

## Steps

1. Acknowledge the indicators of burnout and declining motivation.

2. Ask each person to take some sticky notes and write an answer to the question, "What would get me back on board?"

3. Write the question on a chart as people work.

4. After 5–10 minutes ask everyone to post their notes.

5. Take them one at a time and let each person have a chance to communicate their concern and request.

6. If you are conducting a regular meeting, take the communication as advice, and explain how you intend to follow up. In a special meeting ask the team how it thinks the issues can be addressed.

**RENEWAL**

# Graphic Debriefs

## Be Explicit About What Works!

At the end of intense projects hold a special debriefing meeting to look at what worked, what could be improved, and overall learnings that can support the team next time around. Conducting this session around a large chart illustrating the big stages of the project helps focus the discussion, and helps team members see the process in its entirety. Online meetings can focus on a slide review of key stages and use chat or white board. Acknowledgements and commendations for special efforts are easy to integrate into this practice. Taking time to learn strengthens a team and makes the next challenge less daunting.

## Tips

*Pick a facilitator for this session who was not closely involved.*

*Keep the discussion observational. If people generalize, ask for specifics.*

*On a troubled project, this session may start slowly and will accelerate as people feel the release of tensions during communication.*

## Steps

1. Mark columns for major stages of a project on a large chart.

2. Divide these into three rows; from the top, label them "What Worked?," "What Can We Improve?" and "Learnings."

3. Explain that the session's purpose is to learn and do better next time, not to blame. Set explicit ground rules.

4. Begin each phase with "What worked?" Shift to "What can we improve?" second.

5. Ask for general learnings or guiding principles and chart them along the bottom.

6. Have a little social celebration at the end of the session.

# Accomplishments Review

## *Acknowledge Successes*

At the end of a project or task every team needs to take time to recognize its group and individual accomplishments. The completed process needs to be turned into stories and descriptions that become the "testimonial" for that activity. This provides a positive ending for the team or a transition and motivation for the next round of teamwork. If the team is to stay together, follow this practice with a "next-steps" practice linked to a new task or project.

**Renewal**

**Time**
30 minutes

## Tips

*The more festive you make this, the more powerful it can be. Try decorating the room to make the environment specific to the occasion.*

*Limit the number of milestones so that the detail is filled in by the team.*

*Use different colored markers for the different categories so that they can easily be read.*

*A real party is a good follow-up for really big accomplishments.*

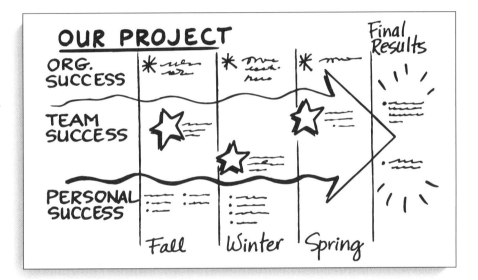

## Steps

1. Hang a large sheet of poster paper or create a simple template in a web-conference program.

2. Mark off the time involved in the project.

3. Spend a few minutes remembering key events.

4. Record all successes/results.

5. Cover personal, team and organization-wide accomplishments.

**RENEWAL**

# Storytelling

**Renewal**

**Time**

2 hours

### Share the History of Your Experience

Looking back over all the work the team has accomplished in a formal review session provides a chance for everyone to get acknowledged. These sessions can be conducted with graphic support, creating a visual case study of the team process that can be shared with others, or can be supported by special slide shows created in preparation for a web conference. Tape recording the session generates a transcript or a written case that can live on in training materials.

## Tips

*Use simple, stan-
dard graphics
for the history,
such as circles
for meetings and
arrows for
projects.*

*Interview some-
one in advance
if you are unac-
quainted with
the story and
want to work out
chart techniques.*

*Consider video-
taping the ses-
sion. People usu-
ally have special
things to say.*

## Steps

1.  Make sure key team players attend the meeting in which you intend to conduct the review.

2.  Hang up a large sheet of paper with a timeline the length of the project.

3.  Interview the team about its experience, starting with the events that initially triggered the process.

4.  Record key events as they are mentioned.

5.  Let the story take over. Use the chart to capture highlights.

6.  Ask questions to get people to elaborate.

7.  Invite the team to review the story and identify key principles that could apply to future team processes.

# Special Recognition

## Acknowledge What You Have Learned from Others

At the end of processes that have stretched a team to new levels of performance, take time to let people share what they have gained from each other. This can be done formally in writing or informally in an open exchange. Suggest this practice as an acknowledgement event, not an evaluation. Once started, this kind of exchange usually takes on a life of its own. There is always a huge amount of learning that occurs in any working team.

**Renewal**

**Time**
1 hour

## Tips
*Be prepared for this session to become somewhat emotional.*

*Include smaller as well as larger learnings so that everyone is included.*

## Steps

1. Invite people to acknowledge what they have learned from each other over the course of the project.

2. Keep the invitation open to any relevant level of learning.

3. Model the process by sharing something you have learned from someone.

4. Facilitate the session until everyone who wishes has shared what they felt they learned.

5. As you end, summarize the benefits you believe the team has gained as a result of its work together.

**RENEWAL**

# Ritual Closings

**Renewal**

**Time**
.5–1 hour

## Complete Events on a Special Note

Take time at the end of meetings and projects to mark the moment in a special way. Gather in a circle and acknowledge the people who arranged the meeting, or invite closing comments and acknowledgements. Hold special meals and make special awards to people who have contributed in ways that serve as models for others. Giving people time to really feel the ending of a process clears the way for beginning anew.

### Tips

*Closings suggested by the team itself will have more buy-in.*

*Remember that transitions involve feelings, and people have many different ways of expressing themselves.*

*Remain sensitive to cultural conditioning that may unintentionally exclude some people.*

## Steps

1. Allocate time at the end of an important meeting or team process for a closing.

2. Invite several team members to think up an appropriate closing. Encourage creativity. Be sensitive to cultural differences.

3. At the appropriate time have people move to some kind of arrangement of chairs or positions that suggests a special event, such as a circle.

4. Explain the approach or invite the planning group to introduce the event.

5. Make sure everyone has a chance to participate.

# Celebrations

## *Mark Completions with Special Events*

Stop periodically to appreciate all of your team's work and accomplishments. Planning special celebrations can get everyone involved and build a real sense of relationship that carries over into the next project. Celebrations can mark endings, beginnings, or milestones along the way. Each stage of process benefits by having a bridge to the next one. This practice has no limits in terms of how celebration is expressed. Just do it!

## Tips

*Celebrating personal victories can be important to a team.*

*Hold your celebrations in special settings if possible; include important symbols, guests, and remembrances.*

## Steps

1. Identify special accomplishments or milestones that deserve celebration.

2. Organize a special subcommittee to plan the celebration.

3. Get everyone's input ahead of time to ensure involvement.

4. Schedule the celebration at a time when people can enjoy it.

5. Invite key leaders and other key stakeholders to attend.

6. Let the team get the glory.

# Using the Practices with Dispersed Teams

Most of the best practices described in this sourcebook apply to dispersed teams. In fact, the use of structured collaborative practices can add a vitality and clarity to remote work that is often missing in informal, ad hoc processes. And the use of graphic frameworks, in the absence of the visual stimuli of face-to-face meetings, provides a clear focal point for exchanges and literally gets team members on the same page. Here are some guidelines for using the practices in virtual space:

**Practices for "different time, different place" meetings (via e-mail and shared websites)**

1. Use pre-work documents on a portal or as an e-mail attachment to prepare for interactive, real-time sessions.

2. If you are conducting any of the practices through a threaded conversation in a portal, take time to insert summaries and overview comments to support movement toward action and results.

3. Provide clear navigation aids that show links and locations of key source documents.

4. Provide members with explicit guidelines regarding response deadlines and send reminders via e-mail to encourage involvement.

5. If a practice involves a graphic framework for gathering input, you might want to generate inputs through teleconferences or web conferences, and then post successive versions of the framework on a portal so everyone can reference the same common image and experience as "being on the same page."

**Practices for "same time, different place" meetings (via teleconference, web conference, or video conference).**

1. Take time to think through what will be dealt with in regularly scheduled meetings and what will require special, focused meetings.

2. When you schedule a meeting or set up a specific practice as an agenda item, provide members with a summary of the process and any expectations regarding their participation in advance, so that they can be prepared. (Fax a page from this book.)

3. Work from a specific agenda and set of desired outcomes that you have circulated in advance.

4. Provide a brief check-in period at the beginning that allows team members to reconnect with each other since participants will be joining the meeting without the social context provided by getting together face to face.

5. Establish a protocol that ensures that each member has an opportunity to speak if you want to encourage full participation. This can be as simple as agreeing on an order for speaking (the equivalent of going around the table) or creating a digital seating chart with pictures sent in advance of the meeting.

6. Get subteams involved in planning presentations for web conferences in advance through teleconferences.

7. Actively manage the time for presentations and discussions.

8. If the process will be supported by a graphic framework for capturing input, ideas or conclusions, consider how to introduce and use the graphic. Some options are:

   a. If the meeting will be held by audio conference, send a copy of the graphic to the members in advance, so it can be used to frame the exchange.
   b. If the meeting will be held by web conference, display the graphic using an appropriate application, ideally one that can be used to record member contributions as they are offered. Using a video camera or a Tablet PC to capture and broadcast the graphic as a team member records responses works well if bandwidth isn't a constraint for participants. Otherwise use an application that allows you to type responses onto the graphic template.

9. Use chat and polling to break up the monotony of slides and talking.

*10.* Provide plenty of emotional breaks—by doing wacky things like throwing virtual tomatoes at people (a function allowed in "Virtual classroom"), or playing music into the speaker phone through a boom box, or having everyone answer some kind of whimsical question.

*11.* End meetings with a summary of decisions taken and actions agreed upon.

*12.* Follow up the meeting by distributing a written summary of the decisions and actions and updating your team portal, if you have one, to reflect the results of the meeting.

**Practices that extend over the life of the team**

A number of the practices involve creating a visual map of the team's work. (See *History Mapping*—page 70, *Vision and Bold Steps*—page 100, *Gameplan Posters*—page 128, *Process Maps*—page 130, *Work flow Diagrams*—page 140.) These maps can be extremely valuable with dispersed teams, to help you provide a graphic context for everyone's work—something that is easily lost as your team members respond to the work pressures of their own location. Once these charts or slides are developed they can be posted on the team portal, referred to in team meetings and updated as the work of the team evolves. Appropriate graphic imagery can help these charts and maps come alive and overcome some of the cultural barriers that words alone might encounter.

Remember that there is no substitute for actually knowing people. Visits and face-to-face kickoff meetings are invaluable for dispersed teams if you can arrange them. Having special encounters through communications media that don't involve work, but are explicitly aimed at getting to know each other, are also very helpful.

As a team leader of a dispersed team, you and your communications become the reliable reference point, instead of a physical office and the cohort group. You have a wide variety of choices for what you can establish that becomes the reliable reference and infrastructure, but you do not really have a choice about needing to establish something. Start with a handful of tried-and-true practices, and then add from there—and don't be afraid to experiment.

# Section III:

## Success Strategies

- Success Strategies: Overview
- Maps to Success Strategies for:
  - —Team Formation
  - —Relationship Building
  - —Stakeholder Enrollment
  - —Goal Alignment
  - —Project Planning
  - —Role Clarification
  - —Decision Making
  - —Progress Review
  - —Conflict Resolution
  - —Creative Problem Solving
  - —Change Management
  - —Action Learning

# Success Strategies: Overview

The previous section of this guide describes more than 80 best practices that you can use with your team. They are keyed to the Team Performance Model so that you can go directly to those options that deal specifically with the challenges of a specific stage. You can think of the practices as "plays" in your team leader "play-book." Often, however, you need more than a specific practice to address a particular situation. You need an overall process for handling a critical phase of the team's work.

As we have seen from the Team Performance Model, there are predictable challenges that essentially all teams face. And for each of these challenges there are proven processes, or success strategies, for helping teams successfully address these challenges. These success strategies are combinations of relevant best practices woven together into integrated "game-plans." The following chart shows the 12 success strategies that are flow-charted in this section. As the "V" shape of the chart indicates, each strategy is linked to the stage of the Team Performance Model that it primarily addresses, though most cover more than one stage.

# Success

**1. Orientation**

**Team Formation**
*(pages 158–159)*

**2. Trust Building**

**Relationship Building**
*(pages 160–161*

**Stakeholder Enrollment**
*(pages 162–163)*

**3. Goal Clarification**

**Goal Alignment**
*(pages 164–165)*

**Project Planning**
*(pages 166–167)*

**4. Commitment**

**Role Clarification**
*(pages 168–169)*

Each success strategy is laid out as a flow chart to assist you in developing the process most appropriate for your team. The column at the left margin provides a quick checklist for assessing whether this strategy is appropriate for your team's current situation. The elements depicted in the flow charts are:

- Circles—showing actions to take

- Diamonds—showing questions you need to answer to determine which branch of the flow chart to follow

- Rectangles—showing best practices found in this guide on the referenced page

- Arrows—showing linkages to other Success Strategies

Use these success strategies as recommendations and suggestions, rather than precise formulas. Customize them to fit the character of your team. Once you have experienced the power of this approach, you will probably want to design some of your own success strategies using other best practices found in this guide and ones that that you have developed yourself.

# trategies

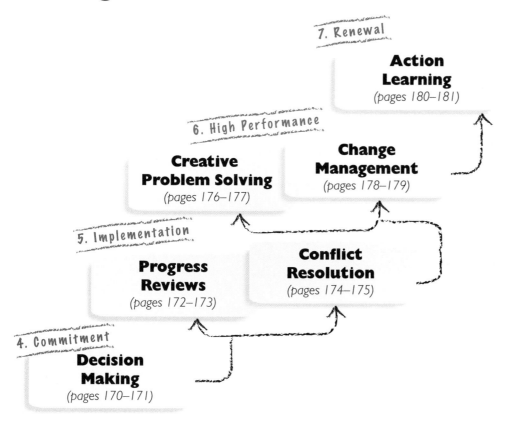

# When should you use TEAM FORMATION?

- **When a new team is being formed**

- **At the beginning of a new project**

- **When several teams are being merged**

- **When a number of new members are being added to the team**

- **When circumstances require that your team realign its direction and goals**

★ BEGIN HERE

*Get Acquainted*
- *Introductions* practice (page 55)
- *Expectations* practice (page 58)

↓

Share the *Big Picture* practice (page 63) and do *Charter Clarification* practice (page 62).

↓

Does your team project have a history?

YES →

Lead team members in *History Mapping* practice (page 70).

NO ↓

Map your current team context. See *Context Mapping* practice (page 85).

*Understand Team Performance*
- Review the *Team Performance Model* practice (page 79)
- Share *Personal Bests* (page 72)

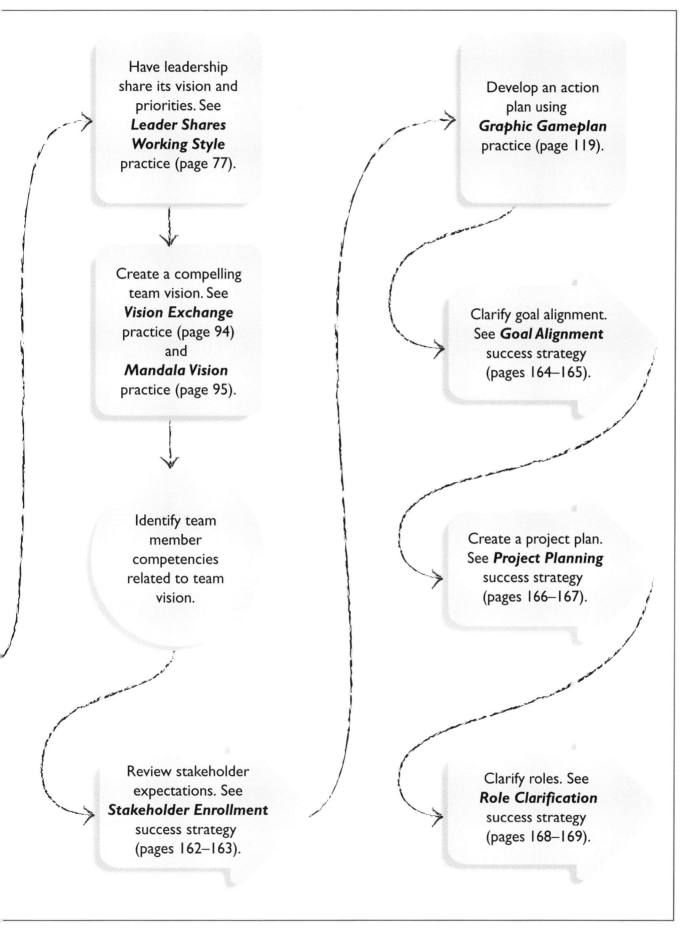

Have leadership share its vision and priorities. See ***Leader Shares Working Style*** practice (page 77).

Create a compelling team vision. See ***Vision Exchange*** practice (page 94) and ***Mandala Vision*** practice (page 95).

Identify team member competencies related to team vision.

Review stakeholder expectations. See ***Stakeholder Enrollment*** success strategy (pages 162–163).

Develop an action plan using ***Graphic Gameplan*** practice (page 119).

Clarify goal alignment. See ***Goal Alignment*** success strategy (pages 164–165).

Create a project plan. See ***Project Planning*** success strategy (pages 166–167).

Clarify roles. See ***Role Clarification*** success strategy (pages 168–169).

# When should you use RELATION- SHIP BUILDING?

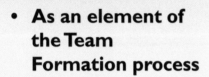

- **As an element of the Team Formation process**

- **When adding new team members**

- **When all members of a dispersed team are together face to face**

- **When team member relationships need support or renewal**

★ BEGIN HERE

Assess what relationship-building activities are within/outside the acceptable norms of the team. Activities to consider include:

Working together on team challenges in ways that encourage new patterns of relating. See:
- *Dialogues* practice (page 76)
- *Customer Visits* practice (page 141)
- *Team-based Problem Solving* practice (page 138)
- *Pop-Up Sessions* practice (page 137)

Activities focused on learning new skills, knowledge, ways of working together. See:
- *Meeting Evaluations* practice (page 135)
- *Personal Bests* practice (page 72)
- *Sharing Backgrounds* practice (page 69)
- *Learning Games* practice (page 75)

Task assignments that the whole team works on together. See:
- *History Mapping* practice (page 70)
- *SPOT Analysis* practice (page 90)
- *Context Mapping* practice (page 85)

Social events based on team interest. Consider:
- Cooking a meal together
- Participating in a volunteer public benefit activity
- Participating in a fun and challenging activity that requires teamwork

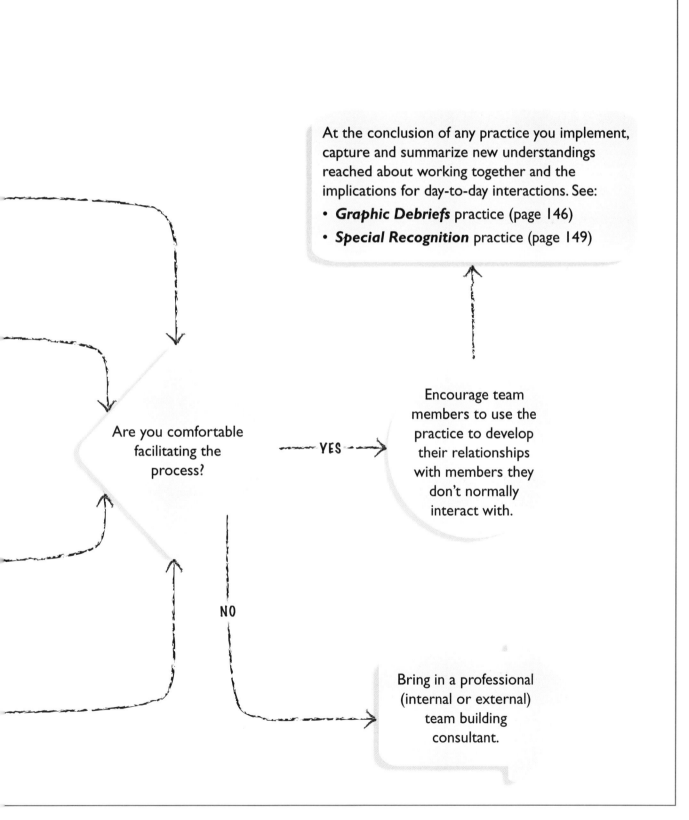

At the conclusion of any practice you implement, capture and summarize new understandings reached about working together and the implications for day-to-day interactions. See:
- *Graphic Debriefs* practice (page 146)
- *Special Recognition* practice (page 149)

Encourage team members to use the practice to develop their relationships with members they don't normally interact with.

Are you comfortable facilitating the process?

----- YES ----->

NO

Bring in a professional (internal or external) team building consultant.

# When should you use STAKEHOLDER ENROLLMENT?

- **When your team's success depends heavily on the support of key stakeholders**

- **When your team is becoming isolated and out of touch**

- **When you suspect there will be substantial benefit gained by linking the work of your team more closely with other work going on**

- **When some of your stakeholders are asking to be more involved**

**BEGIN HERE**

Identify key stakeholders using **Stakeholder Map** practice (page 78).

Identify those stakeholders who are critical to the success of this project/goal.

Assess the needs and interests of those stakeholders.

Determine the appropriate level of involvement by those stakeholders in your team's planning process.

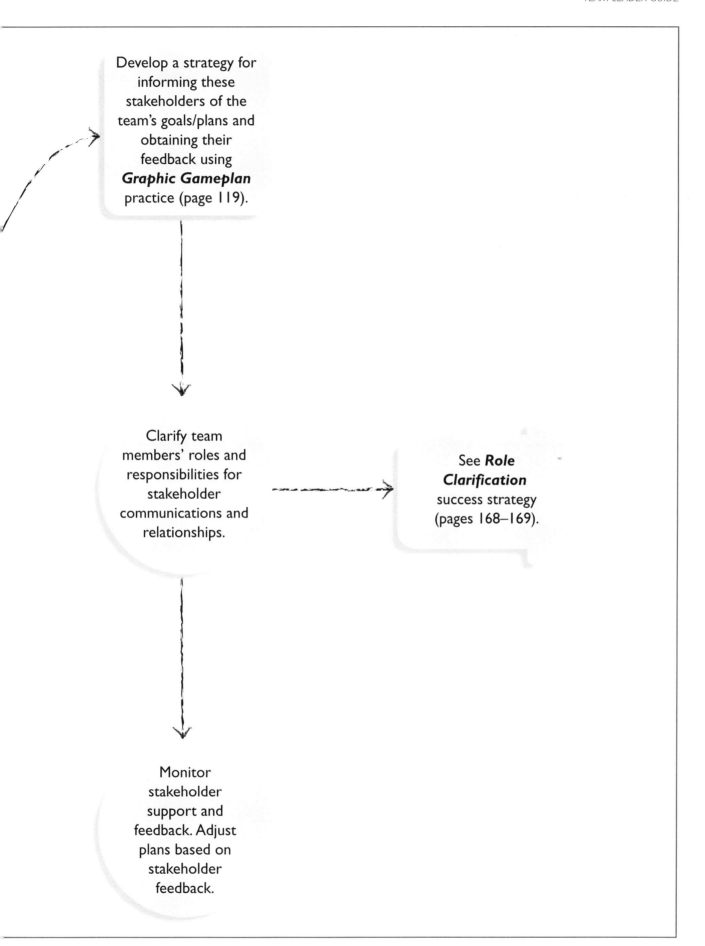

Develop a strategy for informing these stakeholders of the team's goals/plans and obtaining their feedback using **Graphic Gameplan** practice (page 119).

Clarify team members' roles and responsibilities for stakeholder communications and relationships.

See **Role Clarification** success strategy (pages 168–169).

Monitor stakeholder support and feedback. Adjust plans based on stakeholder feedback.

# When should you use GOAL ALIGNMENT?

- **During your organization's regular planning process**

- **When the organization has made a significant shift in its overall priorities**

- **When you see evidence that there is a misalignment between your team's priorities and those with whom your team needs to work**

- **When the team is out of sync with its downstream customers**

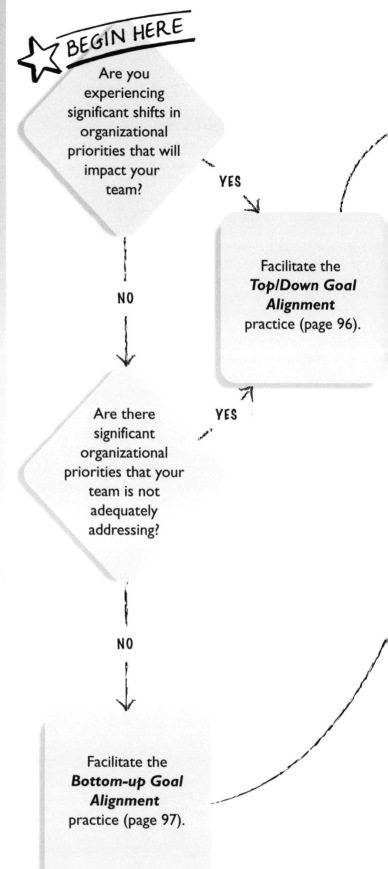

BEGIN HERE

Are you experiencing significant shifts in organizational priorities that will impact your team?

YES

NO

Facilitate the *Top/Down Goal Alignment* practice (page 96).

Are there significant organizational priorities that your team is not adequately addressing?

YES

NO

Facilitate the *Bottom-up Goal Alignment* practice (page 97).

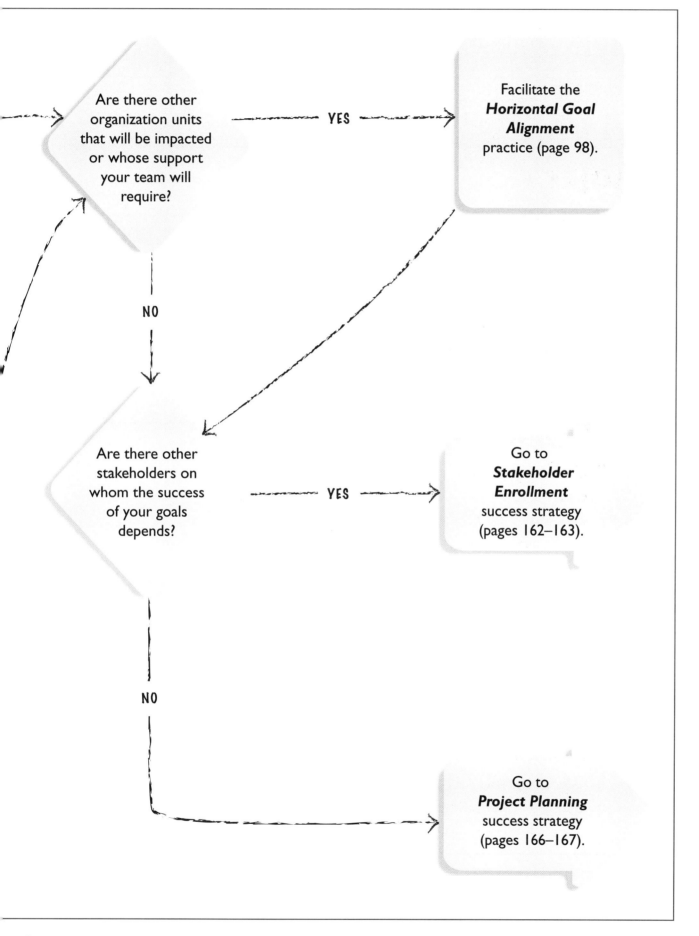

Are there other organization units that will be impacted or whose support your team will require?

YES → Facilitate the *Horizontal Goal Alignment* practice (page 98).

NO

Are there other stakeholders on whom the success of your goals depends?

YES → Go to *Stakeholder Enrollment* success strategy (pages 162–163).

NO

Go to *Project Planning* success strategy (pages 166–167).

# When should you use PROJECT PLANNING?

- **To translate a high-level charter, goal or action plan into a detailed project plan with actions tied to a calendar**

- **To identify important milestones in a long-term project**

- **To provide a clear framework for establishing team member roles and responsibilities**

- **To provide a clear framework for budgeting and resource allocation**

YES

⭐ **BEGIN HERE**

Have you facilitated a high-level *Graphic Gameplan* practice (page 119) or received a charter for your team?

NO

Facilitate a *Graphic Gameplan* practice (page 119) to clarify targets.

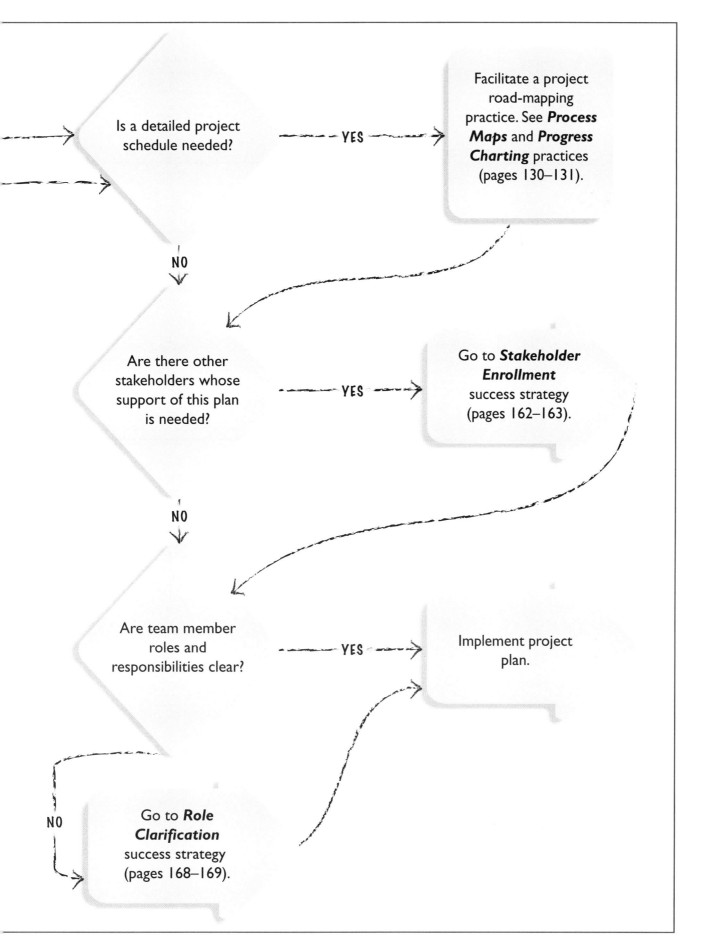

Is a detailed project schedule needed?

YES → Facilitate a project road-mapping practice. See **Process Maps** and **Progress Charting** practices (pages 130–131).

NO

Are there other stakeholders whose support of this plan is needed?

YES → Go to **Stakeholder Enrollment** success strategy (pages 162–163).

NO

Are team member roles and responsibilities clear?

YES → Implement project plan.

NO → Go to **Role Clarification** success strategy (pages 168–169).

# When should you use ROLE CLARIFICATION?

- **To establish a clear understanding among team members of each person's responsibilities**

- **To clarify how team members will work together on interdependent tasks**

- **To resolve any misunderstandings or issues regarding roles and responsibilities among team members**

- **To resolve any matrix issues resulting from dual responsibilities of team members to this team and to their own organizational unit**

 **BEGIN HERE**

Have team members complete **Role Alignment** practice (page 116).

Use results of assessment to identify areas needing clarification.

Is your team's work consistent enough that specific responsibilities can be worked out by the team as a whole?

— YES —

NO

Delegate or decide on role resolution.

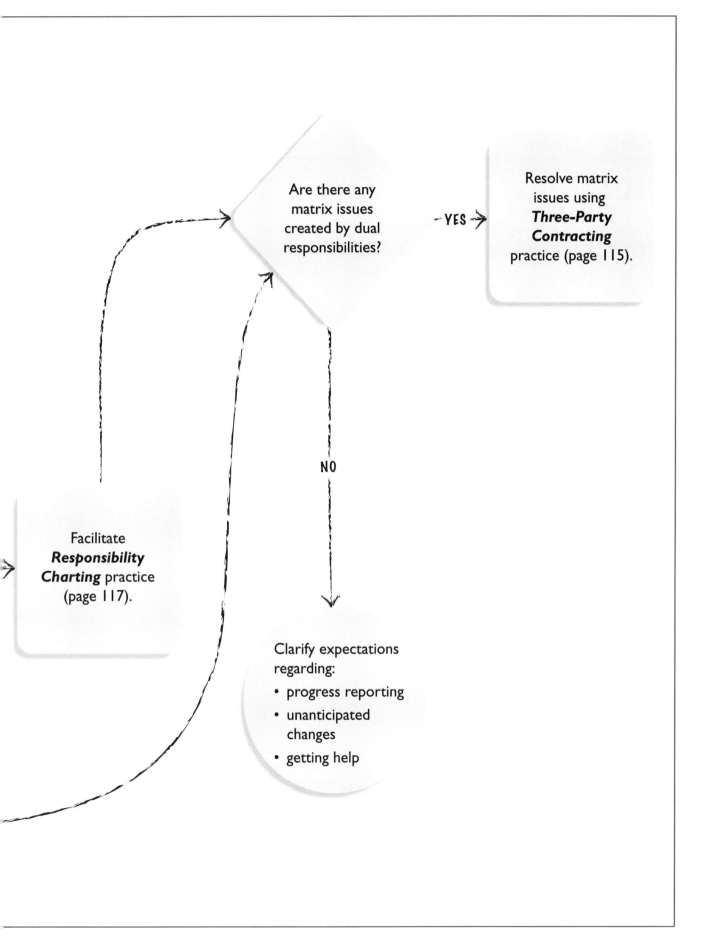

Are there any matrix issues created by dual responsibilities?

Resolve matrix issues using **_Three-Party Contracting_** practice (page 115).

- YES →

NO

Facilitate **_Responsibility Charting_** practice (page 117).

Clarify expectations regarding:
- progress reporting
- unanticipated changes
- getting help

# When should you use DECISION MAKING?

- **To clarify how decisions will be made on your team**

- **To test your team's readiness to make an important decision**

- **To choose a course of action from among a number of viable options**

- **To test the level of commitment to a course of action among team members**

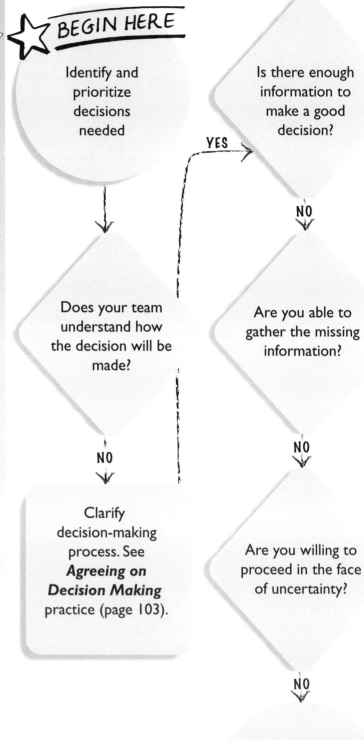

BEGIN HERE

Identify and prioritize decisions needed

Does your team understand how the decision will be made?

NO

Clarify decision-making process. See **Agreeing on Decision Making** practice (page 103).

YES

Is there enough information to make a good decision?

NO

Are you able to gather the missing information?

NO

Are you willing to proceed in the face of uncertainty?

NO

Assess your risk and determine the best course of action.

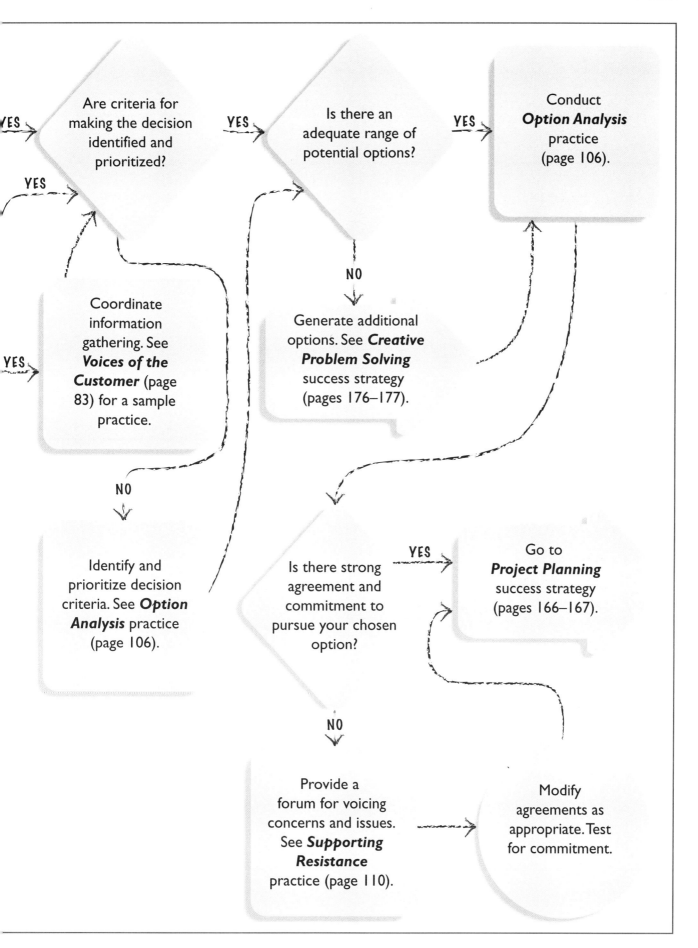

**YES** → Are criteria for making the decision identified and prioritized?

**YES** →

**YES** → Is there an adequate range of potential options?

**YES** →

**YES** → Conduct **Option Analysis** practice (page 106).

**YES** → Coordinate information gathering. See **Voices of the Customer** (page 83) for a sample practice.

**NO** ↓ Generate additional options. See **Creative Problem Solving** success strategy (pages 176–177).

**NO** ↓ Identify and prioritize decision criteria. See **Option Analysis** practice (page 106).

Is there strong agreement and commitment to pursue your chosen option?

**YES** → Go to **Project Planning** success strategy (pages 166–167).

**NO** ↓ Provide a forum for voicing concerns and issues. See **Supporting Resistance** practice (page 110).

Modify agreements as appropriate. Test for commitment.

# When should you use PROGRESS REVIEWS?

- **At the completion of a key milestone**

- **At a pre-established review point**

- **When key indicators are off target**

- **When key stakeholders need to be updated**

- **When new conditions require a size-up of the current situation**

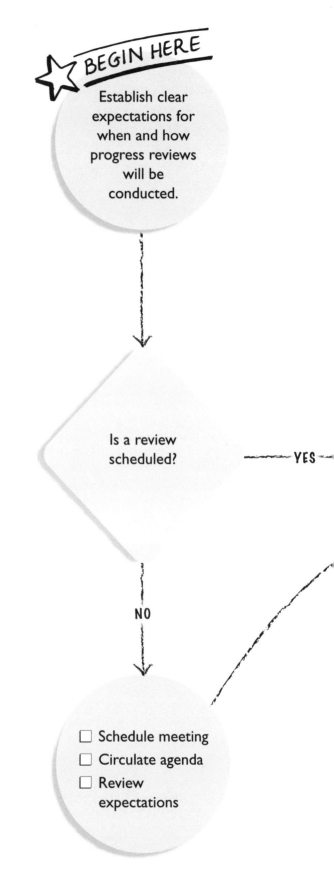

**BEGIN HERE**

Establish clear expectations for when and how progress reviews will be conducted.

Is a review scheduled?

YES

NO

☐ Schedule meeting
☐ Circulate agenda
☐ Review expectations

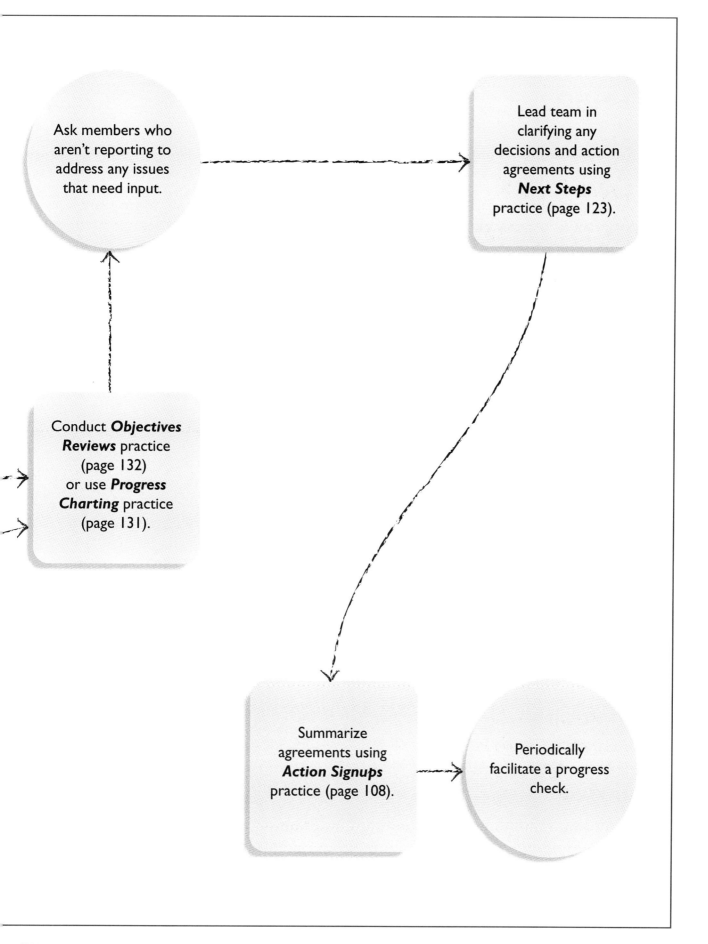

Ask members who aren't reporting to address any issues that need input.

Lead team in clarifying any decisions and action agreements using **Next Steps** practice (page 123).

Conduct **Objectives Reviews** practice (page 132) or use **Progress Charting** practice (page 131).

Summarize agreements using **Action Signups** practice (page 108).

Periodically facilitate a progress check.

# When should you use CONFLICT RESOLUTION?

- **When there is either overt or covert conflict between team members**

- **When there is conflict between your team and others important to the success of your team**

- **When conditions likely to prompt a conflict arise**

- **When you are in conflict with a member of your team**

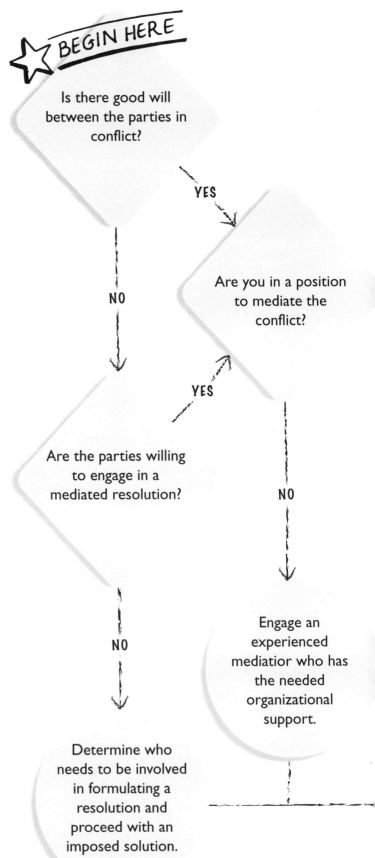

**BEGIN HERE**

Is there good will between the parties in conflict?

YES

NO

Are you in a position to mediate the conflict?

Are the parties willing to engage in a mediated resolution?

YES

NO

NO

Determine who needs to be involved in formulating a resolution and proceed with an imposed solution.

Engage an experienced mediatior who has the needed organizational support.

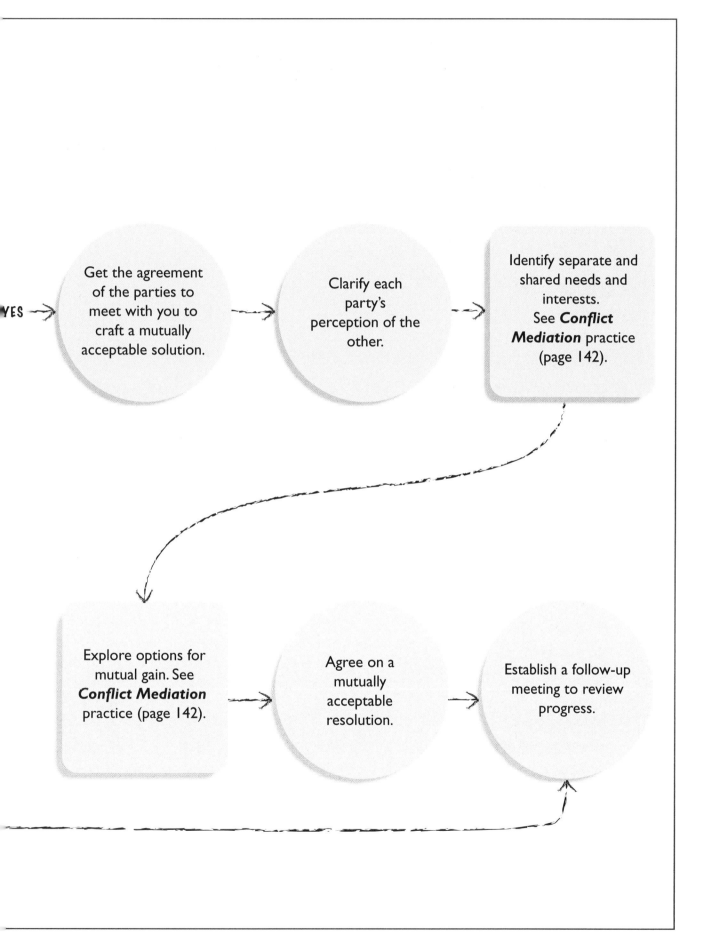

**YES** →

Get the agreement of the parties to meet with you to craft a mutually acceptable solution.

Clarify each party's perception of the other.

Identify separate and shared needs and interests.
See **Conflict Mediation** practice (page 142).

Explore options for mutual gain. See **Conflict Mediation** practice (page 142).

Agree on a mutually acceptable resolution.

Establish a follow-up meeting to review progress.

# When should you use CREATIVE PROBLEM SOLVING?

- **When you need to identify the cause of a persistent problem**

- **When you need to find a creative solution to a new challenge**

- **When you want to engage the best collective thinking of your team**

- **When you want to identify a new approach that can break an impasse**

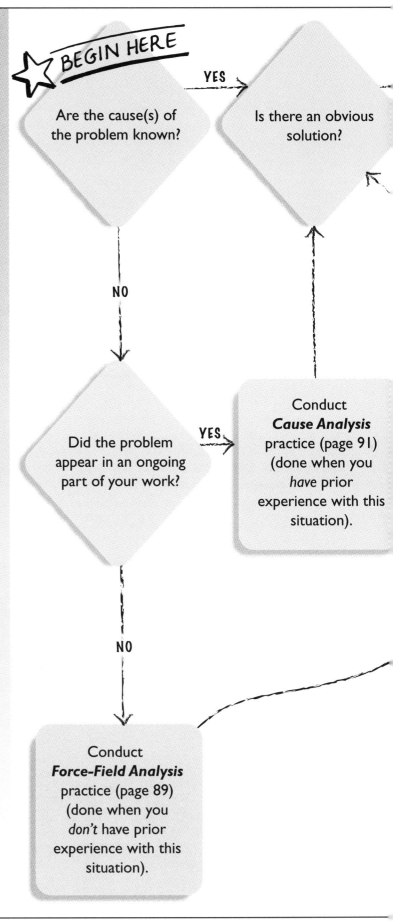

BEGIN HERE

Are the cause(s) of the problem known?

YES

Is there an obvious solution?

NO

Did the problem appear in an ongoing part of your work?

YES

Conduct *Cause Analysis* practice (page 91) (done when you *have* prior experience with this situation).

NO

Conduct *Force-Field Analysis* practice (page 89) (done when you *don't* have prior experience with this situation).

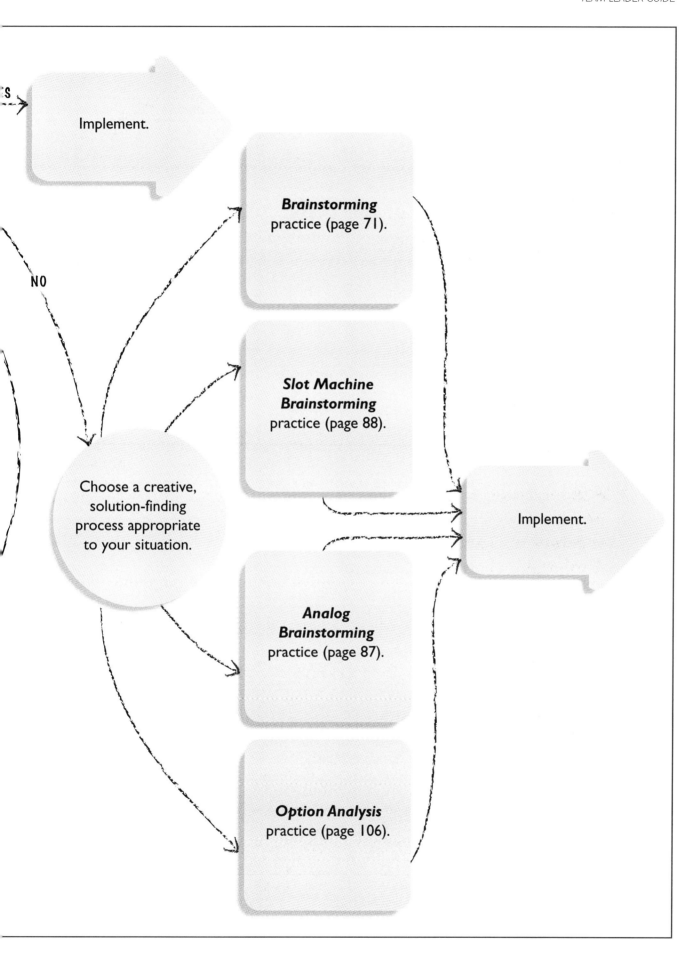

Implement.

Brainstorming
practice (page 71).

NO

Slot Machine
Brainstorming
practice (page 88).

Choose a creative,
solution-finding
process appropriate
to your situation.

Implement.

Analog
Brainstorming
practice (page 87).

Option Analysis
practice (page 106).

# When should you use CHANGE MANAGEMENT?

- **When an unanticipated disruption requires that the team change or modify its approach**

- **When there is not an obvious resolution to an impending change**

- **When you believe it is important to engage the whole team in formulating its response to a change**

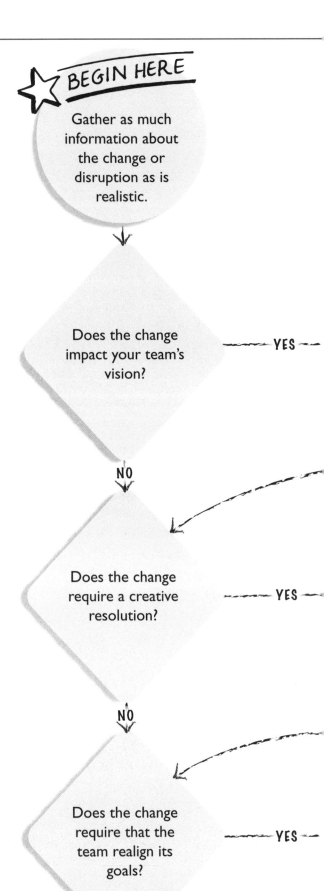

BEGIN HERE

Gather as much information about the change or disruption as is realistic.

Does the change impact your team's vision? — YES —

NO

Does the change require a creative resolution? — YES —

NO

Does the change require that the team realign its goals? — YES —

— NO —

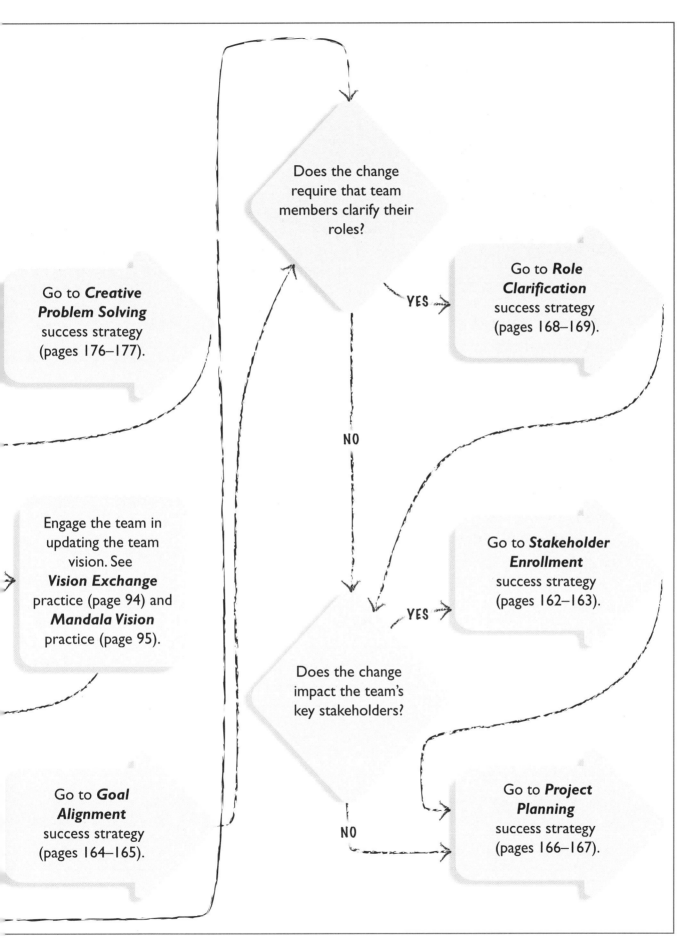

Does the change require that team members clarify their roles?

YES → Go to **Role Clarification** success strategy (pages 168–169).

NO

Go to **Creative Problem Solving** success strategy (pages 176–177).

Engage the team in updating the team vision. See **Vision Exchange** practice (page 94) and **Mandala Vision** practice (page 95).

Go to **Stakeholder Enrollment** success strategy (pages 162–163).

Does the change impact the team's key stakeholders?

YES → Go to **Stakeholder Enrollment** success strategy (pages 162–163).

NO → Go to **Project Planning** success strategy (pages 166–167).

Go to **Goal Alignment** success strategy (pages 164–165).

Go to **Project Planning** success strategy (pages 166–167).

# When should you use ACTION LEARNING?

- **When you want to capture and share knowledge gained directly from first-hand experience**

- **When you want to build team capabilities by taking a calculated action and learning from the results**

- **When the potential benefits of testing a new approach outweigh the risks of failure**

- **When your team has a task that involves a new approach or could lead to unanticipated results**

*Looking Forward*

**BEGIN HERE**

Identify critical team challenges that need creative attention.

Use the **Graphic Gameplan** practice (page 119) to brainstorm an action plan for learning.

*Looking Backward*

**BEGIN HERE**

Set aside a time for your team to explore what they have learned from a success or failure.

Engage your team in telling the story of what happened (avoid blaming or criticism). Conduct **Accomplishments Review** practice(page 147).

Conduct a **Graphic Debrief practice** (page 146).

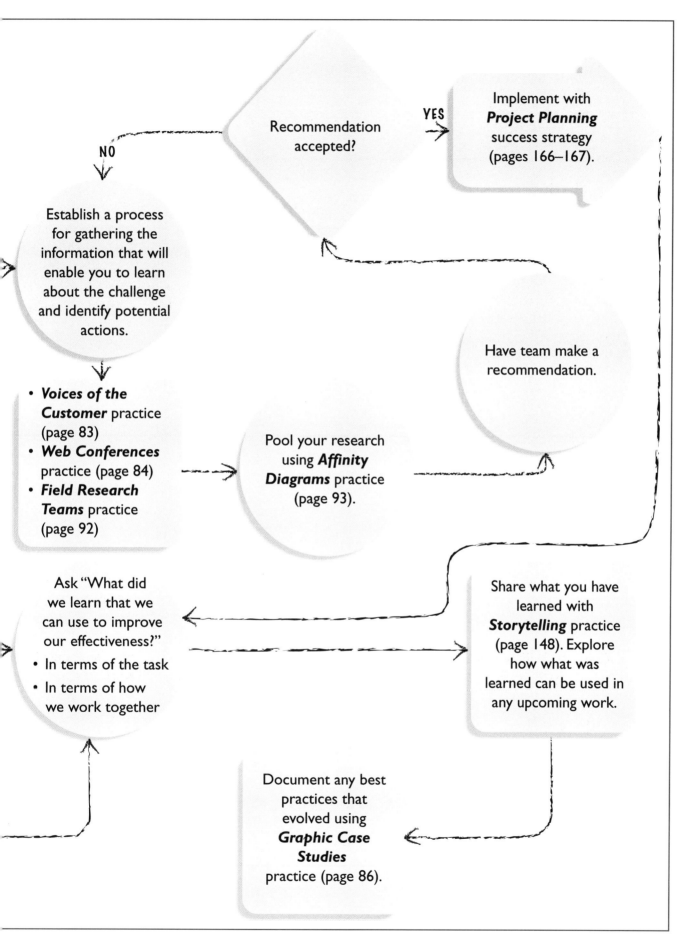

Recommendation accepted?

**YES** → Implement with ***Project Planning*** success strategy (pages 166–167).

**NO** ↓

Establish a process for gathering the information that will enable you to learn about the challenge and identify potential actions.

↓

- ***Voices of the Customer*** practice (page 83)
- ***Web Conferences*** practice (page 84)
- ***Field Research Teams*** practice (page 92)

Pool your research using ***Affinity Diagrams*** practice (page 93).

Have team make a recommendation.

Ask "What did we learn that we can use to improve our effectiveness?"
- In terms of the task
- In terms of how we work together

Share what you have learned with ***Storytelling*** practice (page 148). Explore how what was learned can be used in any upcoming work.

Document any best practices that evolved using ***Graphic Case Studies*** practice (page 86).

# Section IV:

## Self-Guided Team Leadership Development

- Assessing Your Team Leadership Competencies

- Developing Your Team Leader Capabilities

# Assessing Your Team Leadership Competencies

A valuable starting point for developing your skills as a team leader is to complete an assessment of your current skill level. This will help you to target your development work to get the greatest payoff in effectiveness.

The following checklist organizes a set of team leader competencies around the fundamental stages of team development you will be responsible for managing, as contained in the Drexler/Sibbet Team Performance Model described earlier (see pages 22–35). The checklist includes management skills and facilitation skills. One of the most important aspects of leading a team is knowing when to take full charge and when to facilitate your team members in working through issues together. This dual role of manager/facilitator is described in greater detail on page 37.

### You Can Share This Assessment Too

This assessment is designed for you to do an individual, realistic appraisal of your proficiency in each area listed. But everyone has blind spots and biases in different areas. If you are willing to do so, you can broaden your own assessment by having several others complete it. These can be people who have observed you in a variety of situations, like a boss, spouse, close friend, co-workers, or subordinates. If you want to do this, copy the assessment before you fill it out.

### Instructions

1. On the assessment, place a check in the appropriate box following each item to indi-cate how capable you are of using the described skill.

   - Check High if you are able to use the skill effectively in challenging situations

   - Check the fourth box if you are able to use the skill in most normal situations

   - Check the middle box if you are able to use the basic elements of the skill

   - Check the second box if you have only a basic understanding but no real experience using the skill

   - Check the Low box if you are unfamiliar with the skill

2. Next, rate the importance of the skill to your success in your team leader role.

   - L (Low)—not important to your effectiveness

   - M (Medium)—useful but not critical to your effectiveness

   - H (High)—can have a major impact on your effectiveness

3. Use the skills you rated high in competency as a guide to the kinds of practices you might be very proficient at using initially. Your lower rated skills indicate which stages in team performance might need further development. The following section describes how you might go about this.

| Team Leader Skills Assessment | Current Competency Level | | | | | Importance to Your Job |
|---|---|---|---|---|---|---|
| | Low ◄─────────► High | | | | | L / M / H |

### 1. ORIENTATION—CLARIFYING PURPOSE—Why are we a team?

| | | | | | | | |
|---|---|---|---|---|---|---|---|
| 1. | Stating your purpose clearly | ☐ | ☐ | ☐ | ☐ | ☐ | |
| 2. | Clarifying needs and outcomes | ☐ | ☐ | ☐ | ☐ | ☐ | |
| 3. | Proposing strategies for achieving success | ☐ | ☐ | ☐ | ☐ | ☐ | |
| 4. | Reframing negative viewpoints | ☐ | ☐ | ☐ | ☐ | ☐ | |
| 5. | Supporting exploration of win/win outcomes | ☐ | ☐ | ☐ | ☐ | ☐ | |
| 6. | Helping people clarify what is really worth pursuing | ☐ | ☐ | ☐ | ☐ | ☐ | |
| 7. | Creating team charters | ☐ | ☐ | ☐ | ☐ | ☐ | |

### 2. TRUST BUILDING—CONNECTING PEOPLE—Who are we?

| | | | | | | | |
|---|---|---|---|---|---|---|---|
| 8. | Establishing rapport | ☐ | ☐ | ☐ | ☐ | ☐ | |
| 9. | Inviting participation | ☐ | ☐ | ☐ | ☐ | ☐ | |
| 10. | Demonstrating personal integrity and honesty | ☐ | ☐ | ☐ | ☐ | ☐ | |
| 11. | Respecting diversity | ☐ | ☐ | ☐ | ☐ | ☐ | |
| 12. | Helping people share experiences and interests | ☐ | ☐ | ☐ | ☐ | ☐ | |
| 13. | Setting credible expectations | ☐ | ☐ | ☐ | ☐ | ☐ | |
| 14. | Pacing the flow of work so everyone can participate productively | ☐ | ☐ | ☐ | ☐ | ☐ | |
| 15. | Creating space for everyone to contribute | ☐ | ☐ | ☐ | ☐ | ☐ | |
| 16. | Working with resistors to understand their issues and engage their support | ☐ | ☐ | ☐ | ☐ | ☐ | |

### 3. CLARIFYING GOALS—DRAWING OUT INFORMATION—What are we doing?

| | | | | | | | |
|---|---|---|---|---|---|---|---|
| 17. | Asking effective questions | ☐ | ☐ | ☐ | ☐ | ☐ | |
| 18. | Listening for understanding | ☐ | ☐ | ☐ | ☐ | ☐ | |
| 19. | Employing visual tools to support information gathering and processing | ☐ | ☐ | ☐ | ☐ | ☐ | |
| 20. | Establishing clear frameworks that focus attention and energy | ☐ | ☐ | ☐ | ☐ | ☐ | |
| 21. | Engaging skeptics and critics | ☐ | ☐ | ☐ | ☐ | ☐ | |
| 22. | Engaging team members in researching answers to their own questions | ☐ | ☐ | ☐ | ☐ | ☐ | |
| 23. | Clarifying options | ☐ | ☐ | ☐ | ☐ | ☐ | |

### 4. COMMITTING TO DIRECTION—GETTING CLOSURE—How will we work together?

| | | | | | | | |
|---|---|---|---|---|---|---|---|
| 24. | Proposing clear decision processes | ☐ | ☐ | ☐ | ☐ | ☐ | |

| Team Leader Skills Assessment, *continued* | Current Competency Level | | | | | Importance to Your Job |
|---|---|---|---|---|---|---|
| | Low ◄─────────► High | | | | | L / M / H |
| 25. Clarifying decision criteria | ☐ | ☐ | ☐ | ☐ | ☐ | |
| 26. Testing for consensus | ☐ | ☐ | ☐ | ☐ | ☐ | |
| 27. Testing for level of commitment | ☐ | ☐ | ☐ | ☐ | ☐ | |
| 28. Delegating roles and responsibilities | ☐ | ☐ | ☐ | ☐ | ☐ | |
| 29. Crafting win/win agreements | ☐ | ☐ | ☐ | ☐ | ☐ | |
| 30. Addressing competing priorities | ☐ | ☐ | ☐ | ☐ | ☐ | |
| 31. Facilitating the search for creative solutions | ☐ | ☐ | ☐ | ☐ | ☐ | |

### 5. IMPLEMENTATION—SUPPORTING ACTION—*Who does what, when, and where?*

| | | | | | | |
|---|---|---|---|---|---|---|
| 32. Facilitating action planning | ☐ | ☐ | ☐ | ☐ | ☐ | |
| 33. Establishing and clarifying communication agreements | ☐ | ☐ | ☐ | ☐ | ☐ | |
| 34. Creating engaging documentation | ☐ | ☐ | ☐ | ☐ | ☐ | |
| 35. Supporting communication among team members | ☐ | ☐ | ☐ | ☐ | ☐ | |
| 36. Leading or facilitating progress reviews | ☐ | ☐ | ☐ | ☐ | ☐ | |
| 37. Engaging key stakeholders | ☐ | ☐ | ☐ | ☐ | ☐ | |
| 38. Managing by milestones | ☐ | ☐ | ☐ | ☐ | ☐ | |

### 6. HIGH PERFORMANCE—FACILITATING & COACHING—*Sustaining the WOW!*

| | | | | | | |
|---|---|---|---|---|---|---|
| 39. Facilitating check-ins | ☐ | ☐ | ☐ | ☐ | ☐ | |
| 40. Providing strategic feedback to team members | ☐ | ☐ | ☐ | ☐ | ☐ | |
| 41. Coaching for continuous improvement | ☐ | ☐ | ☐ | ☐ | ☐ | |
| 42. Building team capacity through on-the-job training, formal training, or stretch assignments. | ☐ | ☐ | ☐ | ☐ | ☐ | |
| 43. Facilitating conflict resolution | ☐ | ☐ | ☐ | ☐ | ☐ | |
| 44. Managing unanticipated change | ☐ | ☐ | ☐ | ☐ | ☐ | |

### 7. RENEWAL—LEVERAGING LEARNING—*Why continue?*

| | | | | | | |
|---|---|---|---|---|---|---|
| 45. Conducting learning reviews | ☐ | ☐ | ☐ | ☐ | ☐ | |
| 46. Documenting achievements | ☐ | ☐ | ☐ | ☐ | ☐ | |
| 47. Capturing and reinforcing best practices | ☐ | ☐ | ☐ | ☐ | ☐ | |
| 48. Staging celebration and acknowledgement experiences | ☐ | ☐ | ☐ | ☐ | ☐ | |
| 49. Identifying ways to leverage results | ☐ | ☐ | ☐ | ☐ | ☐ | |
| 50. Welcoming and orienting new team members | ☐ | ☐ | ☐ | ☐ | ☐ | |

# Developing Your Team Leader Capabilities

Consider for a moment your skills and abilities that led you to your current position of leadership. They probably include:

- Fundamental knowledge and skills needed by anyone who would take on the kind of work you do

- Specialized knowledge and skills you have developed that have helped you stand out among your peers

- Intuitive understanding of what it takes to be effective, particularly in challenging situations, that represents the art of your job or profession

You learned these through some combination of formal training and hands-on experience, probably with the help of teachers or mentors who shared their wealth of accumulated expertise. You may also have observed role models. Certainly you took on a variety of challenging tasks, which required you to hone and improve your skills and deepen your knowledge. And you likely made your share of mistakes along the way, but rather than view these as defeats, you used them as valuable lessons for the future.

Becoming a skilled team leader is no different. Though some would argue that there is mostly art and little science involved in leading an effective team, there is a lot that can be learned about that special art of bringing out the best in a team. The following process outlines specific steps you can take to become an effective and even outstanding team leader.

## 1. Identify Developmental Priorities

a.  Complete "Assessing Your Team Leadership Competencies," pages 184–186, and have several others who know your work style and abilities also complete the questionnaire.

b.  Compare the results, asking for clarification of any ratings from others that you don't understand.

c.  Highlight the items that have both a high importance rating and substantial opportunity for development.

d.  Put these ratings in the context of your personal aspirations.

☐ How would you like to see your career develop?

_____

_____

_____

_____

_____

☐ What are the skills you are likely to need that will support this development?

_____

_____

_____

_____

_____

☐ Which of these are related to the skills you identified in the previous step?

_____

_____

_____

_____

_____

e.  Identify current challenges in your job that could benefit from enhanced team leader skills.

_____

_____

_____

_____

_____

f.  Which of these are related to the skills you identified in the previous step?

_____
_____
_____
_____
_____

g.  Use the combined considerations in the previous three steps to select not more than five competencies that you believe are worth focused developmental effort on your part.

_____
_____
_____
_____
_____

## 2. Identify Development Opportunities

Now that you have targeted specific competencies that you intend to build and enhance, the next step is to identify opportunities to work on them.

*   Personal Learning Style: How do you prefer to learn new information and skills? Check the items that apply.

    ☐ Interaction with others?

    ☐ By yourself?

    ☐ Learn what you can and then apply it?

    ☐ Try something out and then learn from the results?

    ☐ Working with an experienced teacher or mentor?

    ☐ Mastering a skill before exposing it to the scrutiny of experienced critics?

What are the implications of your preferred style for how you want to approach the development of your team leader skills?

_____
_____
_____
_____

1.
2.
3.
4.
5.

## DEVELOPMENT OPPORTUNITIES

Check over these four areas where you might find development opportunities, and identify options that you can work into a gameplan on the following page.

### Formal Training Opportunities

☐ What formal training does your organization provide or support that addresses the skills you have targeted?

_____
_____
_____
_____
_____

☐ What self-study resources or books are relevant?

_____
_____
_____
_____
_____

☐ Who can help you locate these resources?

_____
_____
_____
_____
_____

### On-the-Job Learning Opportunities

☐ In addition to your normal job, what special assignments or tasks would give you the opportunity to work on your team leader skills? (Consider things you are already involved with first, such as planning and facilitating your manager's next planning session rather than simply participating.)

_____
_____
_____
_____
_____

☐ Which of these tasks could you ask your manager to let you do?

_____
_____
_____
_____
_____

### Coaching/Mentoring Resources

☐ Who would you consider to be a valuable coach or mentor with regard to your team leader capabilities?

_____
_____
_____
_____

☐ Does your organization support or encourage mentoring relationships? Yes___ No___

☐ How can you go about asking for this kind of support?

_____
_____
_____
_____

### Away-from-work Opportunities

You are probably involved in team or group activities outside your work environment. These represent opportunities to take on a team leadership role in an environment where you can probably experiment more freely and where the consequences are not as great if things don't go as planned. You can even let your group know that you are working on your leadership skills and ask for their support and feedback.

☐ Identify several non-work opportunities you can imagine yourself taking on:

_____
_____
_____
_____
_____

### 3. Create a Personal, One-Year Development Plan

Review the opportunities you identified on the previous page. Highlight those you are willing to pursue. Use the Graphic Gameplan practice (page 119) and template to lay out your objectives and the actions you intend to take to achieve them, setting down any milestones or key dates you can use to track your progress. Make note of likely obstacles, so you prepare in advance to deal with them. And capture any success factors that will help ensure that you stay disciplined in this learning pursuit.

### 4. Get Your Manager's Support

Your manager is a key stakeholder in your development, and may have asked you to prepare this development plan or may just be pleased that you took the initiative. Either way, your manager can help provide the resources, opportunities, coaching and feedback you will need to be successful. Arrange a meeting to share your plan, invite a critique and suggestions, and ask for endorsement.

## Leadership Development Gameplan

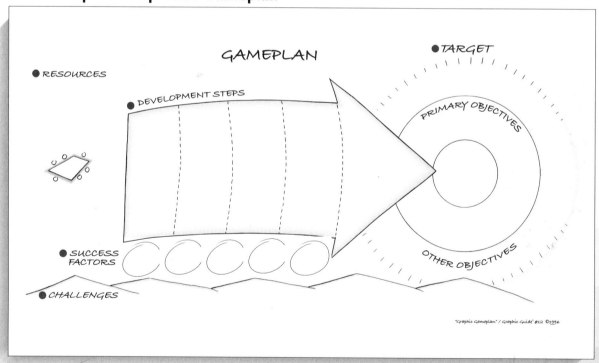

"Graphic Gameplan" / Graphic Guide" #12 ©1996